Anonymous

Women Novelists of Queen Victoria's Reign

A Book of Appreciations

Anonymous

Women Novelists of Queen Victoria's Reign
A Book of Appreciations

ISBN/EAN: 9783337026820

Printed in Europe, USA, Canada, Australia, Japan

Cover: Foto ©Thomas Meinert / pixelio.de

More available books at **www.hansebooks.com**

Women Novelists
Of
Queen Victoria's Reign

A Book of Appreciations

By

Mrs. Oliphant, Mrs. Lynn Linton
Mrs. Alexander, Mrs. Macquoid, Mrs. Parr
Mrs. Marshall, Charlotte M. Yonge
Adeline Sergeant & Edna Lyall

London
Hurst & Blackett, Limited
13 Great Marlborough Street
1897

CONTENTS

THE SISTERS BRONTË
    By Mrs. Oliphant   *Page* 1

GEORGE ELIOT
    By Mrs. Lynn Linton   *Page* 61

MRS. GASKELL
    By Edna Lyall   *Page* 117

MRS. CROWE
MRS. ARCHER CLIVE
MRS. HENRY WOOD
    By Adeline Sergeant   *Page* 149

LADY GEORGIANA FULLERTON
MRS. STRETTON
ANNE MANNING
    By Charlotte M. Yonge   *Page* 193

CONTENTS

DINAH MULOCK (MRS. CRAIK)
    By Mrs. Parr   Page 217

JULIA KAVANAGH
AMELIA BLANDFORD EDWARDS
    By Mrs. Macquoid   Page 249

MRS. NORTON
    By Mrs. Alexander   Page 275

"A. L. O. E." (MISS TUCKER)
MRS. EWING
    By Mrs. Marshall   Page 291

PUBLISHERS' NOTE

*H*AVING *been concerned for many years in the publication of works of fiction by feminine writers, it has occurred to us to offer, as our contribution to the celebration of "the longest Reign," a volume having for its subject leading Women Novelists of the Victorian Era.*

In the case of living lady fictionists, it is too early to assess the merit or forecast the future of their works. The present book, therefore, is restricted to Women Novelists deceased.

It was further necessary to confine the volume within reasonable limits, and it was decided, consequently, that it should deal only with Women who did all their work in Fiction after the accession of the Queen. This decision excludes not only such writers as Lady Morgan, Mrs. Opie, Miss Ferrier, Miss Mitford, Mrs. Shelley, and Miss Jane Porter, who, although

PUBLISHERS' NOTE

they died after 1837, published all their most notable stories early in the century; but also such writers as Mrs. Gore, Mrs. Bray, Mrs. S. C. Hall, Mrs. Trollope, Lady Blessington, and Mrs. Marsh, who made their débuts as novelists between 1823 and 1834.

As regards some of the last-named, it might be urged that the works they produced have now no interest other than historical, and can be said to live only so far as they embody more or less accurate descriptions of Society early in the Reign. The "Deerbrook" and "The Hour and the Man" of Miss Martineau are still remembered, and, perhaps, still read; but it is as a political economist and miscellaneous writer, rather than as a Novelist, that their author ranks in literature; while of the tales by Miss Pardoe, Miss Geraldine Jewsbury, and others once equally popular, scarcely the titles are now recollected.

On the other hand, the eminence and permanence of the Brontës, George Eliot, and Mrs. Gaskell are universally recognised; the popularity of Mrs. Craik and Mrs. Henry Wood is still admittedly great; the personality of Mrs. Norton will always send students to her works; Mrs. Crowe and Mrs. Clive were

PUBLISHERS' NOTE

pioneers in domestic and " sensational" fiction; Lady Georgiana Fullerton produced a typical religious novel; Miss Manning made pleasing and acceptable the autobiographico-historical narrative; the authors of " The Valley of a Hundred Fires," of " Barbara's History," and of " Adèle," have even now their readers and admirers; while " A. L. O. E." and Mrs. Ewing were among the most successful caterers for the young.

It has seemed to us that value as well as interest would attach to critical estimates of, and biographical notes upon, these representative Novelists, supplied by living mistresses of the craft; and we are glad to have been able to secure for the purpose, the services of the contributors to this volume, all of whom may claim to discourse with some authority upon the art they cultivate. It is perhaps scarcely necessary to say that each contributor is responsible only for the essay to which her name is appended.

THE SISTERS BRONTË

By MRS. OLIPHANT

THE SISTERS BRONTË

THE effect produced upon the general mind by the appearance of Charlotte Brontë in literature, and afterwards by the record of her life when that was over, is one which it is nowadays somewhat difficult to understand. Had the age been deficient in the art of fiction, or had it followed any long level of mediocrity in that art, we could have comprehended this more easily. But Charlotte Brontë appeared in the full flush of a period more richly endowed than any other we know of in that special branch of literature, so richly endowed, indeed, that the novel had taken quite fictitious importance, and the names of Dickens and Thackeray ranked almost higher than those of any living writers except perhaps Tennyson, then young and on his promotion too. Anthony Trollope and Charles Reade who, though in their day extremely popular, have never had justice from

THE SISTERS BRONTË

a public which now seems almost to have forgotten them, formed a powerful second rank to these two great names. It is a great addition to the value of the distinction gained by the new comer that it was acquired in an age so rich in the qualities of the imagination.

But this only increases the wonder of a triumph which had no artificial means to heighten it, nothing but genius on the part of a writer possessing little experience or knowledge of the world, and no sort of social training or adventitious aid. The genius was indeed unmistakable, and possessed in a very high degree the power of expressing itself in the most vivid and actual pictures of life. But the life of which it had command was seldom attractive, often narrow, local, and of a kind which meant keen personal satire more than any broader view of human existence. A group of commonplace clergymen, intense against their little parochial background as only the most real art of portraiture, intensified by individual scorn and dislike, could have made them : the circle of limited interests, small emulations, keen little spites and rancours, filling the atmosphere of a great boarding school, the Brussels *Pensionnat des filles*—these were the two spheres chiefly portrayed : but portrayed with an absolute untempered force which knew neither charity, softness, nor even impartiality, but burned upon the paper and made everything round

By MRS. OLIPHANT

dim in the contrast. I imagine it was this extraordinary naked force which was the great cause of a success, never perhaps like the numerical successes in literature of the present day, when edition follows edition, and thousand thousand, of the books which are the favourites of the public: but one which has lived and lasted through nearly half a century, and is even now potent enough to carry on a little literature of its own, book after book following each other not so much to justify as to proclaim and echo to all the winds the fame originally won. No one else of the century, I think, has called forth this persevering and lasting homage. Not Dickens, though perhaps more of him than of any one else has been dealt out at intervals to an admiring public; not Thackeray, of whom still we know but little; not George Eliot, though her fame has more solid foundations than that of Miss Brontë. Scarcely Scott has called forth more continual droppings of elucidation, explanation, remark. Yet the books upon which this tremendous reputation is founded though vivid, original, and striking in the highest degree, are not great books. Their philosophy of life is that of a schoolgirl, their knowledge of the world almost *nil*, their conclusions confused by the haste and passion of a mind self-centred and working in the narrowest orbit. It is rather, as we have said, the most incisive and realistic art of portraiture than any exercise of the nobler arts of fiction—imagination, combination, construction—or humorous survey of life or deep apprehension of its problems—upon which this fame is built.

The curious circumstance that Charlotte Brontë was, if the word may be so used, doubled by her sisters, the elder, Emily, whose genius has been taken for granted, carrying the wilder elements of the common inspiration to extremity in the strange, chaotic and weird romance of "Wuthering Heights," while Anne diluted such powers of social observation as were in the family into two mildly disagreeable novels of a much commoner order, has no doubt also enhanced the central figure of the group to an amazing degree. They placed her strength in relief by displaying its separate elements, and thus commending the higher skill and larger spirit which took in both, understanding the moors and wild country and rude image of man better than the one, and misunderstanding the common course of more subdued life less than the other. The three together are for ever inseparable; they were homely, lowly, somewhat neglected in their lives, had few opportunities and few charms to the careless eye: yet no group of women, undistinguished by rank, unendowed by beauty, and known to but a limited circle of friends as unimportant as themselves have ever, I think, in the course of history—

By MRS. OLIPHANT

certainly never in this century—come to such universal recognition. The effect is quite unique, unprecedented, and difficult to account for; but there cannot be the least doubt that it is a matter of absolute fact which nobody can deny.

These three daughters of a poor country clergyman came into the world early in the century, the dates of their births being 1816, 1818, 1820, in the barest of little parsonages in the midst of the moors—a wild but beautiful country, and a rough but highly characteristic and keen-witted people. Yorkshire is the very heart of England; its native force, its keen practical sense, its rough wit, and the unfailing importance in the nation of the largest of the shires has given it a strong individual character and position almost like that of an independent province. But the Brontës, whose name is a softened and decorated edition of a common Irish name, were not of that forcible race: and perhaps the strong strain after emotion, and revolt against the monotonies of life, which were so conspicuous in them were more easily traceable to their Celtic origin than many other developments attributed to that cause. They were motherless from an early age, children of a father who, after having been depicted as a capricious tyrant,

THE SISTERS BRONTË

seems now to have found a fairer representation as a man with a high spirit and peculiar temper, yet neither unkind to his family nor uninterested in their welfare. There was one son, once supposed to be the hero and victim of a disagreeable romance, but apparent now as only a specimen, not alas, uncommon, of the ordinary ne'er-do-well of a family, without force of character or self-control to keep his place with decency in the world.

These children all scribbled from their infancy as soon as the power of inscribing words upon paper was acquired by them, inventing imaginary countries and compiling visionary records of them as so many imaginative children do. The elder girl and boy made one pair, the younger girls another, connected by the closest links of companionship. It was thought or hoped that the son was the genius of the family, and at the earliest possible age he began to send his effusions to editors, and to seek admission to magazines with the mingled arrogance and humility of a half-fledged creature. But the world knows now that it was not poor Branwell who was the genius of the family; and this injury done him in his cradle, and the evil report of him that everybody gives throughout his life, awakens a certain pity in the mind for the unfortunate youth so unable to keep any supremacy among the girls whom he must have considered his natural inferiors and vassals.

By MRS. OLIPHANT

We are told by Charlotte Brontë herself that he never knew of the successes of his sisters, the fact of their successive publications being concealed from him out of tenderness for his feelings; but it is scarcely to be credited that when the parish knew the unfortunate brother did not find out. The unhappy attempt of Mrs. Gaskell in writing the lives of the sisters to make this melancholy young man accountable for the almost brutal element in Emily Brontë's conception of life, and the strange views of Charlotte as to what men were capable of, has made him far too important in their history; where, indeed, he had no need to have appeared at all, had the family pride consisted, as the pride of so many families does, in veiling rather than exhibiting the faults of its members. So far as can be made out now, he had as little as possible to do with their development in any way.

There was nothing unnatural or out of the common in the youthful life of the family except that strange gift of genius, which though consistent with every genial quality of being, in such a nature as that of Scott, seems in other developments of character to turn all the elements into chaos. Its effect upon the parson's three daughters was, indeed, not of a very wholesome kind. It awakened in them an uneasy sense of superiority which gave double force to every one of the little hardships

THE SISTERS BRONTË

which a girl in a great school of a charitable kind, and a governess in a middle-class house, has to support : and made life harder instead of sweeter to them in many ways, since it was full of the biting experience of conditions less favourable than those of many persons round them whom they could not but feel inferior to themselves.

The great school, which it was Charlotte Brontë's first act when she began her literary career to invest with an almost tragic character of misery, privation, and wrong, was her first step from home. Yorkshire schools did not at that period enjoy a very good reputation in the world, and Nicholas Nickleby was forming his acquaintance with the squalid cruelty of Dotheboys Hall just about the same time when Charlotte Brontë's mind was being filled with the privations and discontents of Lowood. In such a case there is generally some fire where there is so much smoke, and probably Lowood was under no very heavenly *régime* : but at the same time its drawbacks were sharply accentuated by that keen criticism which is suggested by the constant sense of injured worth and consciousness of a superiority not acknowledged. The same feeling pursued her into the situations as governess which she occupied one after another, and in which her indignation at being expected to feel affection for the children put under her charge, forms a curious addition to the other grievances with which fate pursues her life. No doubt there are many temptations in the life of a governess; the position of a silent observer in a household, looking on at all its mistakes, and seeing the imperfection of its management with double force because of the effect they have on herself—especially if she feels herself competent, had she but the power, to set things right—must always be a difficult one. It was not continued long enough, however, to involve very much suffering; though no doubt it helped to mature the habit of sharp personal criticism and war with the world.

At the same time Charlotte Brontë made some very warm personal friendships, and wrote a great many letters to the school friends who pleased her, in which a somewhat stilted tone and demure seriousness is occasionally invaded by the usual chatter of girlhood, to the great improvement of the atmosphere if not of the mind. Ellen Nussey, Mary Taylor, women not manifestly intellectual but sensible and independent without either exaggeration of sentiment or hint of tragic story, remained her close friends as long as she lived, and her letters to them, though always a little demure, give us a gentler idea of her than anything else she has written. Not that there is much charm either of style or subject in them : but there is no sort of bitterness or sense of insufficient appreciation. Nothing can be more usual and commonplace, indeed, than this portion of her life. As in so many cases, the artificial lights thrown upon it by theories formed afterwards, clear away when we examine its actual records, and it is apparent that there was neither exceptional harshness of circumstance nor internal struggle in the existence of the girl who, though more or less in arms against everybody outside—especially when holding a position superior to her own, more especially still when exercising authority over her in any way—was yet quite an easy-minded, not unhappy, young woman at home, with friends to whom she could pour out long pages of what is, on the whole, quite moderate and temperate criticism of life, not without cheerful allusion to now and then a chance curate or other young person of the opposite sex, suspected of "paying attention" to one or other of the little coterie. These allusions are not more lofty or dignified than are similar notes of girls of less exalted pretensions, but there is not a touch in them of the keen pointed pen which afterwards put up the Haworth curates in all their imperfections before the world.

The other sisters at this time in the background, two figures always clinging together, looking almost like one, have no great share in this softer part of Charlotte's life. They were, though so different in character, completely devoted to each other, apparently forming no other friendships, each content with the one other partaker of her every thought. A little literature seems to have been created between them, little chapters of recollection and commentary upon their life, sealed up and put away for three years in each case, to be opened on Emily's or on Anne's birthday alternately, as a pathetic sign of their close unity, though the little papers were in themselves simple in the extreme. Anne too became a governess with something of the same experience as Charlotte, and uttering very hard judgments of unconscious people who were not the least unkind to her. But Emily had no such trials. She remained at home perhaps because she was too uncompromising to be allowed to make the experiment of putting up with other people, perhaps because one daughter at home was indispensable. The family seems to have had kind and trusted old servants, so that the cares of housekeeping did not weigh heavily upon the daughter in charge, and there is no evidence of exceptional hardness or roughness in their circumstances in any way.

In 1842, Charlotte and Emily, aged respectively twenty-six and twenty-four, went to Brussels. Their

THE SISTERS BRONTË

design was "to acquire a thorough familiarity with French," also some insight into other languages, with the view of setting up a school on their own account. The means were supplied by the aunt, who had lived in their house and taken more or less care of them since their mother's death. The two sisters were nearly a year in the Pensionnat Héger, now so perfectly known in every detail of its existence to all who have read "Villette." They were recalled by the death of the kind aunt who had procured them this advantage, and afterwards Charlotte, no one quite knows why, went back to Brussels for a second year, in which all her impressions were probably strengthened and intensified. Certainly a more clear and lifelike picture, scathing in its cold yet fierce light, was never made than that of the white tall Brussels house, its class rooms, its gardens, its hum of unamiable girls, its sharp display of rancorous and shrill teachers, its one inimitable professor. It startles the reader to find—a fact which we had forgotten—that M. Paul Emmanuel was M. Héger, the husband of Madame Héger and legitimate head of the house: and that this daring and extraordinary girl did not hesitate to encounter gossip or slander by making him so completely the hero of her romance. Slander in its commonplace form had nothing to do with such

By MRS. OLIPHANT

a fiery spirit as that of Charlotte Brontë : but it shows her perfect independence of mind and scorn of comment that she should have done this. In the end of '43 she returned home, and the episode was over. It was really the only episode of possible practical significance in her life until we come to the records of her brief literary career and her marriage, both towards its end.

The prospect of the school which the three sisters were to set up together was abandoned ; there was no more talk of governessing. We are not told if it was the small inheritance of the aunt—only, Mr. Clement Shorter informs us, £1500—which enabled the sisters henceforward to remain at home without thought of further effort : but certainly this was what happened. And the lives of the two younger were drawing so near the end that it is a comfort to think that they enjoyed this moment of comparative grace together. Their life was extremely silent, secluded, and apart. There was the melancholy figure of Branwell to distract the house with the spectacle of heavy idleness, drink, and disorder ; but this can scarcely have been so great an affliction as if he had been a more beloved brother. He was not, however, veiled by any tender attempt to cover his follies or wickedness, but openly complained of to all their friends,

THE SISTERS BRONTË

which mitigates the affliction : and they seem to have kept very separate from him, living in a world of their own.

In 1846 a volume of poems by Currer, Ellis, and Acton Bell, was published at their own cost. It had not the faintest success ; they were informed by the publisher that two copies only had been sold, and the only satisfaction that remained to them was to send a few copies to some of the owners of those great names which the enthusiastic young women had worshipped from afar as stars in the firmament. These poems were republished after Charlotte Brontë had attained her first triumph, and people had begun to cry out and wonder over "Wuthering Heights." The history of "Jane Eyre," on the other hand, is that of most works which have been the beginning of a career. It fell into the hands of the right man, the "reader" of Messrs. Smith, Elder and Co., Mr. Williams, a man of great intelligence and literary insight. The first story written by Charlotte Brontë, which was called "The Professor," and was the original of "Villette," written at a time when her mind was very full of the emotions raised by that singular portion of her life, had been rejected by a number of publishers, and was also rejected by Mr. Williams, who found it at once too crude and too *short* for the risks of publication, three volumes at that period being your only possible form for fiction. But he saw the power in it, and begged the author to try again at greater length. She did so; not on the basis of the "Professor" as might have seemed natural—probably the materials were still too much at fever-heat in her mind to be returned to at that moment—but by the story of "Jane Eyre," which at once placed Charlotte Brontë amid the most popular and powerful writers of her time.

I remember well the extraordinary thrill of interest which in the midst of all the Mrs. Gores, Mrs. Marshs, &c.—the latter name is mentioned along with those of Thackeray and Dickens even by Mr. Williams—came upon the reader who, in the calm of ignorance, took up the first volume of "Jane Eyre." The period of the heroine in white muslin, the immaculate creature who was of sweetness and goodness all compact, had lasted in the common lines of fiction up to that time. Miss Austen indeed might well have put an end to that abstract and empty fiction, yet it continued, as it always does continue more or less, the primitive ideal. But "Jane Eyre" gave her, for the moment, the *coup de grace*. That the book should be the story of a governess was perhaps necessary to the circumstances of the writer: and the governess was already a favourite figure in fiction. But generally she was of the beautiful, universally fascinating, all-enduring kind, the amiable blameless creature whose secret merits were never so hidden but that they might be perceived by a keen sighted hero. I am not sure, indeed, that anybody believed Miss Brontë when she said her heroine was plain. It is very clear from the story that Jane was never unnoticed, never failed to please, except among the women, whom it is the instinctive art of the novelist to rouse in arms against the central figure, thus demonstrating the jealousy, spite, and rancour native to their minds in respect to the women who please men. No male cynic was ever stronger on that subject than this typical woman. She cannot have believed it, I presume, since her closest friends were women, and she seems to have had perfect faith in their kindness: but this is a matter of conventional belief which has nothing to do with individual experience. It is one of the doctrines unassailable of the art of fiction; a thirty-ninth article in which every writer of novels is bound to believe.

Miss Brontë did not know fine ladies, and therefore, in spite of herself and a mind the reverse of vulgar, she made the competitors for Mr. Rochester's favour rather brutal and essentially vulgar persons, an error, curiously enough, which seems to have been

By MRS. OLIPHANT

followed by George Eliot in the corresponding scenes in "Mr. Gilfil's Love Story," where Captain Wybrow's *fiancée* treats poor Tiny very much as the beauty in Mr. Rochester's house treats Jane Eyre. Both were imaginary pictures, which perhaps more or less excuses their untruthfulness in writers both so sincere and life-like in treating things they knew. It is amusing to remember that Jane Eyre's ignorance of dress gave a clinching argument to Miss Rigby in the *Quarterly* to decide that the writer was not and could not possibly be a woman. The much larger and more significant fact that no man (until in quite recent days when there have been instances of such effeminate art) ever made a woman so entirely the subject and inspiration of his book, the only interest in it, was entirely overlooked in what was, notwithstanding, the very shrewd and telling argument about the dress.

The chief thing, however, that distressed the candid and as yet unaccustomed reader in "Jane Eyre," and made him hope that it might be a man who had written it, was the character of Rochester's confidences to the girl whom he loved—not the character of Rochester, which was completely a woman's view, but that he should have talked to a girl so evidently innocent of his amours and his mistresses. This, however, I think, though, as we should have thought, a subject so abhorrent to a young woman such as Charlotte Brontë was, was also emphatically a woman's view. A man might have credited another man of Rochester's kind with impulses practically more heinous and designs of the worst kind: but he would not have made him err in that way.

In this was a point of honour which the woman did not understand. It marks a curious and subtle difference between the sexes. The woman less enlightened in practical evil considers less the risks of actual vice; but her imagination is free in other ways, and she innocently permits her hero to do and say things so completely against the code which is binding on gentlemen whether vicious or otherwise that her want of perception becomes conspicuous. The fact that the writer of the review in the *Quarterly* was herself a woman accounts for her mistake in supposing that the book was written if not by a man, by "a woman unsexed;" "a woman who had forfeited the society of her sex." And afterwards, when Mrs. Gaskell made her disastrous statements about Branwell Brontë and other associates of Charlotte's youth, it was with the hope of proving that the speech and manners of the men to whom she had been accustomed were of a nature to justify her in any such misapprehension of the usual manners of gentlemen. It was on the contrary, as I think, only the bold and unfettered imagination of a woman quite ignorant on all such subjects which could have suggested this special error. The mind of such a woman, casting about for something to make her wicked but delightful hero do by way of demonstrating his wickedness, yet preserving the fascination which she meant him to retain, probably hit upon this as the very wickedest thing she could think of, yet still attractive: for is there not a thrill of curiosity in searching out what such a strange being might think or say, which is of itself a strong sensation? Miss Brontë was, I think, the first to give utterance to that curiosity of the woman in respect to the man, and fascination of interest in him—not the ideal man, not Sir Kenneth, too reverent for anything but silent worship—which has since risen to such heights of speculation, and imprints now a tone upon modern fiction at which probably she would have been horrified.

There were numberless stories in those days of guilty love and betrayal, of how "lovely woman stoops to folly," and all the varieties of that endless subject; but it was, except in the comic vein, or with grotesque treatment, the pursuit of the woman by the man, the desire of the lover for the beloved which was the aim of fiction. A true lady of romance walked superior: she accepted (or not)

THE SISTERS BRONTË

the devotion: she stooped from her white height to reward her adorer: but that she herself should condescend to seek him (except under the circumstances of fashionable life, where everybody is in quest of a coronet), or call out for him to heaven and earth when he tarried in his coming, was unknown to the situations of romantic art. When the second of Charlotte Brontë's books appeared, there was accordingly quite a new sensation in store for the public. The young women in "Shirley" were all wild for this lover who, though promised by all the laws of nature and romance, did not appear. They leaned out of their windows, they stretched forth their hands, calling for him—appealing to heaven and earth. Why were they left to wear out their bloom, to lose their freshness, to spend their days in sewing and dreaming, when he, it was certain, was about somewhere, and by sheer perversity of fate could not find the way to them? Nothing was thought of the extra half-million of women in those days; perhaps it had not begun to exist; but that "nobody was coming to marry us, nobody coming to woo" was apparent.

Young ladies like Miss Charlotte Brontë and Miss Ellen Nussey her friend, would have died rather than give vent to such sentiments; but when the one of them to whom that gift was given found that her pen had

By MRS. OLIPHANT

become a powerful instrument in her hand, the current of the restrained feeling burst all boundaries, and she poured forth the cry which nobody had suspected before. It had been a thing to be denied, to be indignantly contradicted as impossible, if ever a lovesick girl put herself forth to the shame of her fellows and the laugh of the world. When such a phenomenon appeared, she was condemned as either bad or foolish by every law: and the idea that she was capable of "running after" a man was the most dreadful accusation that could be brought against a woman. Miss Brontë's heroines, however, did not precisely do this. Shirley and Caroline Helstone were not in love so much as longing for love, clamouring for it, feeling it to be their right of which they were somehow defrauded. There is a good deal to be said for such a view. If it is the most virtuous thing in the world for a man to desire to marry, to found a family, to be the father of children, it should be no shameful thing for a woman to own the same desire. But it is somehow against the instinct of primitive humanity, which has decided that the woman should be no more than responsive, maintaining a reserve in respect to her feelings, subduing the expression, unless in the "once, and only once, and to One only" of the poet.

Charlotte Brontë was the first to overthrow this superstition. Personally I am disposed to stand for the superstition, and dislike all transgression of it. But that was not the view of the most reticent and self-controlled of maidens, the little governess, clad in all the strict proprieties of the period, the parson's daughter despising curates, and unacquainted with other men. In her secret heart, she demanded of fate night and day why she, so full of life and capability, should be left there to dry up and wither; and why Providence refused her the completion of her being. Her heart was not set on a special love; still less was there anything fleshly or sensual in her imagination. It is a shame to use such words in speaking of her, even though to cast them forth as wholly inapplicable. The woman's grievance—that she should be left there unwooed, unloved, out of reach of the natural openings of life: without hope of motherhood: with the great instinct of her being unfulfilled—was almost a philosophical, and entirely an abstract, grievance, felt by her for her kind: for every woman dropped out of sight and unable to attain the manner of existence for which she was created. And I think it was the first time this cry had been heard out of the mouth of a perfectly modest and pure-minded woman, nay, out of the mouth of any woman; for it had nothing to do with the shriek of the Sapphos for love. It was more startling, more confusing to the general mind, than the wail of the lovelorn. The gentle victim of "a disappointment," or even the soured and angered victim, was a thing quite understood and familiar : but not the woman calling upon heaven and earth to witness that all the fates were conspiring against her to cheat her of her natural career.

So far as I can see this was the great point which gave force to Charlotte Brontë's genius and conferred upon her the curious pre-eminence she possesses among the romancers of her time. In this view "Shirley," though I suppose the least popular, is the most characteristic of her works. It is dominated throughout with this complaint. Curates ? Yes, there they are, a group of them. Is that the thing you expect us women to marry ? Yet it is our right to bear children, to guide the house. And we are half of the world, and where is the provision for us ?

This cry disturbed the critic, the reader, the general public in the most curious way ; they did not know what to make of it. Was it a shameless woman who was so crying out ? It is always the easiest way, and one which avoids all complications, to say so, and thus crush every question. But it was scarcely easy to believe this in face of other circumstances. Mrs. Gaskell, as much puzzled as any one, when Charlotte Brontë's short life was over, tried hard to account for it by "environment" as the

THE SISTERS BRONTË

superior persons say, that is by the wicked folly of her brother, and the coarseness of all the Yorkshiremen round; and thus originated in her bewilderment, let us hope without other intention, a new kind of biography, as the subject of it inaugurated an entirely new kind of social revolution. ⚡ The cry of the women indeed almost distressed as well as puzzled the world. The vivid genius still held it, but the ideas were alarming, distracting beyond measure. The *Times* blew a trumpet of dismay; the book was revolution as well as revelation. It was an outrage upon good taste, it was a betrayal of sentiments too widespread to be comfortable. It was indelicate if not immodest. We have outgrown now the very use of this word, but it was a potent one at that period. And it was quite a just reproach. That cry shattered indeed altogether the "delicacy" which was supposed to be the most exquisite characteristic of womankind. The softening veil is blown away, when such exhibitions of feeling are given to the world.

From that period to this is a long step. We have travelled through many years and many gradations of sentiment: and we have now arrived at a standard of opinion by which the "sex-problem" has become the most interesting of questions, the chief occupation of fiction, to be discussed by men and women alike with growing warmth and openness, the immodest and the indelicate being equally and scornfully dismissed as barriers with which Art has nothing to do. My impression is that Charlotte Brontë was the pioneer and founder of this school of romance, though it would probably have shocked and distressed her as much as any other woman of her age.

The novels of Emily and Anne Brontë were published shortly after " Jane Eyre," in three volumes, of which "Wuthering Heights" occupied the first two. I am obliged to confess that I have never shared the common sentiment of enthusiasm for that, to me, unlovely book. The absence of almost every element of sympathy in it, the brutality and misery, tempered only by an occasional gleam of the heather, the freshness of an occasional blast over the moors, have prevented me from appreciating a force which I do not deny but cannot admire. The figure of Heathcliffe, which perhaps has called forth more praise than any other single figure in the literature of the time, does not touch me. I can understand how in the jumble which the reader unconsciously makes, explaining him more or less by Rochester and other of Charlotte Brontë's heroes, he may take his place in a sort of system, and thus have humanities read into him, so to speak, which he does

THE SISTERS BRONTE

not himself possess. But though the horror and isolation of the house is powerful I have never been able to reconcile myself either to the story or treatment, or to the estimate of Emily Brontë's genius held so strongly by so many people. There is perhaps the less harm in refraining from much comment on this singular book, of which I gladly admit the unique character, since it has been the occasion of so many and such enthusiastic comments. To me Emily Brontë is chiefly interesting as the double of her sister, exaggerating at once and softening her character and genius as showing those limits of superior sense and judgment which restrained her, and the softer lights which a better developed humanity threw over the landscape common to them both. We perceive better the tempering sense of possibility by which Charlotte made her rude and almost brutal hero still attractive, even in his masterful ferocity, when we see Emily's incapacity to express anything in *her* hero except perhaps a touch of that tragic pathos, prompting to fiercer harshness still, which is in the soul of a man who never more, whatever he does, can set himself right. This is the one strain of poetry to my mind in the wild conception. There was no measure in the younger sister's thoughts, nor temperance in her methods.

The youngest of all, the gentle Anne, would have no

right to be considered at all as a writer but for her association with these imperative spirits. An ordinary little novelette and a moral story, working out the disastrous knowledge gained by acquaintance with the unfortunate Branwell's ruinous habits, were her sole productions. She was the element wanting in Emily's rugged work and nature. Instead of being two sisters constantly entwined with each other, never separate when they could help it, had Anne been by some fantastic power swamped altogether and amalgamated with her best beloved, we may believe that Emily might then have shown herself the foremost of the three. But the group as it stands is more interesting than any single individual could be. And had Charlotte Brontë lived a long and triumphant life, a fanciful writer might have imagined that the throwing off of those other threads of being so closely attached to her own had poured greater force and charity into her veins. But we are baffled in all our suggestions for the amendment of the ways of Providence.

The melancholy and tragic year, or rather six months, which swept from Haworth Parsonage three of its inmates, and left Charlotte and her father alone to face life as they might, was now approaching; and it seems so completely an episode in the story of the elder sister's genius as well as her life, that its history is like that of an unwritten tragedy, hers as much as her actual work. Branwell was the first to die, unwept yet not without leaving a pathetic note in the record. Then came the extraordinary passion and agony of Emily, which has affected the imagination so much, and which, had it been for any noble purpose, would have been a true martyrdom. But to die the death of a Stoic, in fierce resistance yet subjection to Nature, regardless of the feelings of all around, for the sake of pride and self-will alone, is not an act to be looked upon with the reverential sympathy which, however, it has secured from many. The strange creature with her shoes on her feet and her staff in her hand, refusing till the last to acknowledge herself to be ill or to receive any help in her weakness, gives thus a kind of climax to her strange and painful work. Her death took place in December of the same year (1848) in which Branwell died. Anne, already delicate, would never seem to have held up her head after her sister's death, and in May 1849 she followed, but in all sweetness and calmness, to her early grave. She was twenty-eight; Emily twenty-nine. So soon had the fever of life worn itself out and peace come. Charlotte was left alone. There had not been to her in either of them the close companion which they had found in each other. But yet life ebbed away from her with their deaths, which occurred in such a startling and quick succession as always makes bereavement more terrible.

This occurred at the height of her mental activity. "Shirley" had been published, and had been received with the divided feeling we have referred to ; and when she was thus left alone she found, no doubt, the solace which of all mortal things work gives best, by resuming her natural occupation in the now more than ever sombre seclusion of the Parsonage, to which, however, her favourite friend, Ellen Nussey, came from time to time. One or two visits to London occurred after the two first publications in which, a demure little person, silent and shy, yet capable of expressing herself very distinctly by times, and by no means unconscious of the claim she now had upon other people's respect and admiration, Charlotte Brontë made a little sensation in the society which was opened to her, not always of a very successful kind. Everybody will remember the delightfully entertaining chapter in literary history in which Mrs. Ritchie, with charming humour and truth, recounts the visit of this odd little lion to her father's house, and Thackeray's abrupt and clandestine flight to his club when it was found that nothing more was to be made of her than an absorbed conversation with the governess in the back drawing-room, a situation like one in a novel, and so very like the act of

THE SISTERS BRONTË

modest greatness, singling out the least important person as the object of her attentions.

She is described by all her friends as plain, even ugly—a small woman with a big nose, and no other notable feature, not even the bright eyes which are generally attributed to genius—which was probably, however, better than the lackadaisical portrait prefixed to her biography, after a picture by Richmond, which is the typical portrait of a governess of the old style, a gentle creature deprecating and wistful. Her letters are very good letters, well expressed in something of the old-fashioned way, but without any of the charm of a born letter-writer. Indeed, charm does not seem to have been hers in any way. But she had a few very staunch friends who held fast by her all her life, notwithstanding the uncomfortable experience of being "put in a book," which few people like. It is a gift by itself to put other living people in books. The novelist does not always possess it; to many the realms of imagination are far more easy than the arid realms of fact, and to frame an image of a man much more natural than to take his portrait. I am not sure that it is not a mark of greater strength to be able to put a living and recognisable person on the canvas than it is to invent one. Anyhow, Miss Brontë possessed it in great perfection. Impossible to doubt that the characters of "Shirley" were real men ; still more impossible to doubt for a moment the existence of M. Paul Emmanuel. The pursuit of such a system requires other faculties than those of the mere romancist. It demands a very clear-cut opinion, a keen judgment not disturbed by any strong sense of the complexities of nature, nor troubled by any possibility of doing injustice to its victim.

One thing strikes us very strongly in the description of the school, Lowood, which was her very first step in literature, and in which there can now be no doubt, from her own remarks on the manner in which it was received, she had a vindictive purpose. I scarcely know why, for, of course, the dates are all there to prove the difference—but my own conclusion had always been that she was a girl of fourteen or fifteen, old enough to form an opinion when she left the school. I find, with much consternation, that she was only nine; and that so far as such a strenuous opinion was her own at all, it must have been formed at that early and not very judicious age. That the picture should be so vivid with only a little girl's recollection to go upon is wonderful ; but it is not particularly valuable as a verdict against a great institution, its founder and all its ways. Nevertheless, it had its scathing and wounding effect as much as if the little observer, whose small judgment worked so precociously, had been capable of understanding the things which she condemned. It would be rash to trust nineteen in such a report, but nine!

It was at a different age and in other circumstances that Charlotte Brontë made her deep and extraordinary study of the Brussels Pensionnat. She was twenty-seven ; she had already gone through a number of those years of self-repression during which, by dint of keeping silence, the heart burns. She was, if we may accept the freedom of her utterances in fiction as more descriptive of her mind than the measured sentences of her letters, angry with fate and the world which denied her a brighter career, and bound her to the cold tasks of dependence and the company of despised and almost hated inferiors during the best of her life. Her tremendous gift of sight—not second sight or any visionary way of regarding the object before her, but that vivid and immediate vision which took in every detail, and was decisive on every act as if it had been the vision of the gods—was now fully matured. She saw all that was about her with this extraordinary clearness without any shadow upon the object or possibility of doubt as to her power of seeing it all round and through and through. She makes us also see and know the big white house, with every room distinct : the garden, with its great trees and alleys : the class-rooms, each with its tribune : the girls, fat and round and phlegmatic in characteristic foreignism, and herself as spectator, looking on with contemptuous indifference, not caring to discriminate beween them. The few English figures, which concern her more, are drawn keen upon the canvas, though with as little friendliness; the teachers sharply accentuated, Mdlle. Sophie, for instance, who, when she is in a rage, has no lips, and all the sharp contentions and false civilities of those banded Free Lances, enemies to everybody and to each other ; the image of watchful suspicion in the head of the house—all these are set forth in glittering lines of steel. There is not a morsel of compunction in the picture. Everybody is bad, worthless, a hater of the whole race. The mistress of the establishment moves about stealthily, watching, her eyes showing through a mist in every corner, going and coming without a sound. What a picture it is ! There is not a good meaning in the whole place—not even that beneficent absence of meaning which softens the view. They are all bent on their own aims, on gaining an advantage great or small over their neighbours ; nobody is spared, nobody is worth a revision of judgment—except one.

The little Englishwoman herself, who is the centre of all this, is not represented as more lovable than the rest.

THE SISTERS BRONTË

She is the hungry little epicure, looking on while others feast, and envying every one of them, even while she snarls at their fare as apples of Gomorrah. She cannot abide that they should be better off than she, even though she scorns their satisfaction in what they possess. Her wild and despairing rush through Brussels when the town is *en fête*, cold, impassioned, fever-hot with rancour and loneliness, produces the most amazing effect on the mind. She is the banished spirit for whom there is no place, the little half-tamed wild beast, wild with desire to tear and rend everything that is happy. One feels that she has a certain justification and realises the full force of being left out in the cold, of having no part or lot in the matter when other people are amused and rejoice. Many other writers have endeavoured to produce a similar effect with milder means, but I suppose because of a feeble-minded desire to preserve the reputation of their forlorn heroine and give the reader an amiable view of her, no one has succeeded like the author of "Villette," who is in no way concerned for the amiability of Lucy Snowe.

For the impartiality of this picture is as extraordinary as its power. Lucy Snowe is her own historian; it is the hot blood of the autobiographist that rushes through her veins, yet no attempt is made to recommend her to the reader or gain his sympathy. She is much too real to think of these

By MRS. OLIPHANT

outside things, or of how people will judge her, or how to make her proceedings acceptable to their eyes. We do not know whether Charlotte Brontë ever darted out of the white still house, standing dead in the moonlight, and rushed through the streets and, like a ghost, into the very heart of the gaslights and festivities; but it would be difficult to persuade any reader that some one had not done so, imprinting that phantasmagoria of light and darkness upon a living brain. Whether it was Charlotte Brontë or Lucy Snowe, the effect is the same. We are not even asked to feel for her or pity her, much less to approve her. Nothing is demanded from us on her account but merely to behold the soul in revolt and the strange workings of her despair. It was chiefly because of the indifference to her of Dr. John that Lucy was thus driven into a momentary madness; and with the usual regardless indiscretion of all Charlotte Brontë's amateur biographers, Mr. Shorter intimates to us who was the living man who was Dr. John and occasioned all the commotion. The tragedy, however it appears, was unnecessary, for the victim got over it with no great difficulty, and soon began the much more engrossing interest which still remained behind.

Nothing up to this point has attracted us in " Villette," except, indeed, the tremendous vitality and reality of the whole, the sensation of the actual which is in every line, and which forbids us to believe for a moment that what we are reading is fiction. But a very different sentiment comes into being as we become acquainted with the black bullet-head and vivacious irascible countenance of M. Paul Emmanuel. He is the one only character in Miss Brontë's little world who has a real charm, whose entrance upon the stage warms all our feelings and awakens in us not interest alone, but lively liking, amusement and sympathy. The quick-witted, quick-tempered Frenchman, with all the foibles of his vanity displayed, as susceptible to any little slight as a girl, as easily pleased with a sign of kindness, as far from the English ideal as it is possible to imagine, dancing with excitement, raging with displeasure, committing himself by every step he takes, cruel, delightful, barbarous and kind, is set before us in the fullest light, intolerable but always enchanting. He is as full of variety as Rosalind, as devoid of dignity as Pierrot, contradictory, inconsistent, vain, yet conquering all our prejudices and enchanting us while he performs every antic that, according to our usual code, a man ought not to be capable of. How was it that for this once the artist got the better of all her restrictions and overcame all her misconceptions, and gave us a man to be heartily loved, laughed at, and taken into our hearts?

By MRS. OLIPHANT

I cannot answer that question. I am sorry that he was M. Héger, and the master of the establishment, and not the clever tutor who had so much of Madame Beck's confidence. But anyhow, he is the best that Miss Brontë ever did for us, the most attractive individual, the most perfect picture. The Rochesters were all more or less fictitious, notwithstanding the unconscious inalienable force of realism which gives them, in spite of themselves and us, a kind of overbearing life; but Miss Brontë never did understand what she did not know. She had to see a thing before it impressed itself upon her, and when she did see it, with what force she saw! She knew M. Paul Emmanuel, watching him day by day, seeing all his littlenesses and childishness, his vanity, his big warm heart, his clever brain, the manifold nature of the man. He stands out, as the curates stood out, absolutely real men about whom we could entertain no doubt, recognisable anywhere. The others were either a woman's men, like the Moors of Shirley, whose roughness was bluster (she could not imagine an Englishman who was not rough and rude), and their strength more or less made up; or an artificial composition like St. John, an ideal bully like Rochester. The ideal was not her forte—she had few gifts that way: but she saw with overwhelming lucidity and keenness, and what she saw, without a doubt, without a scruple, she could put upon the canvas in lines of fire. Seldom, very seldom, did an object appear within reach of that penetrating light, which could be drawn lovingly or made to appear as a being to be loved. Was not the sole model of that species M. Paul? It would seem that in the piteous poverty of her life, which was so rich in natural power, she had never met before a human creature in whom she could completely trust, or one who commended himself to her entirely, with all his foibles and weaknesses increasing, not diminishing, the charm.

It is, in my opinion, a most impertinent inquiry to endeavour to search out what were the sentiments of Charlotte Brontë for M. Héger. Any one whom it would be more impossible to imagine as breaking the very first rule of English decorum, and letting her thoughts stray towards another woman's husband, I cannot imagine. Her fancy was wild and her utterance free, and she liked to think that men were quite untrammelled by those proprieties which bound herself like bonds of iron in her private person, and that she might pluck a fearful joy by listening to their dreadful experiences: but she herself was as prim and Puritan as any little blameless governess that ever went out of an English parish. But while believing this I cannot but feel it was an intolerable spite of fortune that the one man whom she knew in her life, whom her story could make others love, the only man whom she saw with that real illumination which does justice to humanity, was not M. Paul Emmanuel but M. Héger. This was why we were left trembling at the end of Lucy Snowe's story, not knowing whether he ever came back to her out of the wilds, fearing almost as keenly that nothing but loss could fitly end the tale, yet struggling in our imaginations against the doom—as if it had concerned our own happiness.

Was this new-born power in her, the power of representing a man at his best, she who by nature saw both men and women from their worst side, a sign of the development of genius in herself, the softening of that scorn with which she had hitherto regarded a world chiefly made up of inferior beings, the mellowing influence of maturity? So we might have said, had it not been that after this climax of production she never spake word more in the medium of fiction. Had she told the world everything she had to say? Could she indeed say nothing but what she had seen and known in her limited experience—the trials of school and governessing, the longing of women, the pangs of solitude? That strange form of imagination which can deal only with fact, and depict nothing but what is under its eyes, is in its way perhaps the most impressive of all—especially when inspired by the remorseless lights of that keen out-

THE SISTERS BRONTË

ward vision which is unmitigated by any softening of love for the race, any embarrassing toleration as to feelings and motives. It is unfortunately true in human affairs that those who expect a bad ending to everything, and suspect a motive at least dubious to every action, prove right in a great number of cases, and that the qualities of truth and realism have been appropriated to their works by almost universal consent. Indeed there are some critics who think this the only true form of art. But it is at the same time a power with many limitations. The artist who labours, as M. Zola does, searching into every dust-heap, as if he could find out human nature, the only thing worth depicting, with all its closely hidden secrets, all its flying indistinguishable tones, all its infinite gradations of feeling, by that nauseous process, or by a roaring progress through the winds, upon a railway brake, or the visit of a superficial month to the most complicated, the most subtle of cities—must lay up for himself and for his reader many disappointments and deceptions : but the science of artistic study, as exemplified in him, had not been invented in Charlotte Brontë's day.

She did not attempt to go and see things with the intention of representing them ; she was therefore limited to the representation of those things which naturally in the course of life came under her eyes. She knew, though only as a

By MRS. OLIPHANT

child, the management and atmosphere of a great school, and set it forth, branding a great institution with an insufferable stigma, justly or unjustly, who knows? She went to another school and turned out every figure in it for our inspection—a community all jealous, spiteful, suspicious, clandestine: even the chance pupil with no particular relation to her story or herself, painted with all her frivolities for the edification of the world did not escape. "She was Miss So-and-So," say the army of commentators who have followed Miss Brontë, picking up all the threads, so that the grand-daughter of the girl who had the misfortune to be in the Brussels Pensionnat along with that remorseless artist may be able to study the character of her ancestress. The public we fear loves this kind of art, however, notwithstanding all its drawbacks.

On the other hand probably no higher inspiration could have set before us so powerfully the image of M. Paul. Thus we are made acquainted with the best and the worst which can be effected by this method—the base in all their baseness, the excellent all the dearer for their characteristic faults: but the one representation scarcely less offensive than the other to the victim. Would it be less trying to the individual to be thus caught, identified, written out large in the light of love and glowing adoration, than in the more natural light of scorn? I know not indeed which would be

THE SISTERS BRONTË

the worst ordeal to go through, to be drawn like Madame Beck, suspicious, stealthy, with watchful eyes appearing out of every corner, surprising every incautious word, than to be put upon the scene in the other manner, with all your peccadilloes exposed in the light of admiration and fondness, and yourself put to play the part of hero and lover. The point of view of the public is one thing, that of the victim quite another. We are told that Miss Brontë, perhaps with a momentary compunction for what she had done, believed herself to have prevented all injurious effects by securing that "Villette" should not be published in Brussels, or translated into the French tongue, both of them of course perfectly futile hopes since the very desire to hinder its appearance was a proof that this appearance would be of unusual interest. The fury of the lady exposed in all her stealthy ways could scarcely have been less than the confusion of her spouse when he found himself held up to the admiration of his town as Lucy Snowe's captivating lover. To be sure it may be said the public has nothing to do with this. These individuals are dead and gone, and no exposure can hurt them any longer, whereas the gentle reader lives for ever, and goes on through the generations, handing on to posterity his delight in M. Paul. But all the same it is a cruel and in reality an immoral art; and it has this great

By MRS. OLIPHANT

disadvantage, that its area is extremely circumscribed, especially when the artist lives most of her life in a Yorkshire parsonage amid the moors, where so few notable persons come in her way.

There was however one subject of less absolute realism which Charlotte Brontë had at her command, having experienced in her own person and seen her nearest friends under the experience, of that solitude and longing of women, of which she has made so remarkable an exposition. The long silence of life without an adventure or a change, the forlorn gaze out at windows which never show any one coming who can rouse the slightest interest in the mind, the endless years and days which pass and pass, carrying away the bloom, extinguishing the lights of youth, bringing a dreary middle age before which the very soul shrinks, while yet the sufferer feels how strong is the current of life in her own veins, and how capable she is of all the active duties of existence—this was the essence and soul of the existence she knew best. Was there no help for it? Must the women wait and long and see their lives thrown away, and have no power to save themselves?

The position in itself so tragic is one which can scarcely be expressed without calling forth an inevitable ridicule, a laugh at the best, more often a sneer at the women whose desire for a husband is thus betrayed. Shirley and Caroline Helston both cried out for that husband with an indignation, a fire and impatience, a sense of wrong and injury, which stopped the laugh for the moment. It might be ludicrous but it was horribly genuine and true. Note there was nothing sensual about these young women. It was life they wanted; they knew nothing of the grosser thoughts which the world with its jeers attributes to them: of such thoughts they were unconscious in a primitive innocence which perhaps only women understand. They wanted their life, their place in the world, the rightful share of women in the scheme of nature. Why did not it come to them? The old patience in which women have lived for all the centuries fails now and again in a keen moment of energy when some one arises who sees no reason why she should endure this forced inaction, or why she should invent for herself inferior ways of working and give up her birthright, which is to carry on the world.

The reader was horrified with these sentiments from the lips of young women. The women were half ashamed, yet more than half stirred and excited by the outcry, which was true enough if indelicate. All very well to talk of women working for their living, finding new channels for themselves, establishing their independence. How much have we said of all that, endeavouring to persuade ourselves! Charlotte Brontë had the courage of her opinions. It was not education nor a trade that her women wanted. It was not a living but their share in life, a much more legitimate object had that been the way to secure it, or had there been any way to secure it in England. Miss Brontë herself said correct things about the protection which a trade is to a woman, keeping her from a mercenary marriage; but this was not in the least the way of her heroines. They wanted to be happy, no doubt, but above all things they wanted their share in life—to have their position by the side of men, which alone confers a natural equality, to have their shoulder to the wheel, their hands on the reins of common life, to build up the world, and link the generations each to each. In her philosophy marriage was the only state which procured this, and if she did not recommend a mercenary marriage she was at least very tolerant about its conditions, insisting less upon love than was to be expected and with a covert conviction in her mind that if not one man then another was better than any complete abandonment of the larger path. Lucy Snowe for a long time had her heart very much set on Dr. John and his placid breadth of Englishism: but when she finally found out that to be impossible her tears were soon dried by the prospect of Paul Emmanuel, so unlike him, coming into his place.

THE SISTERS BRONTË

Poor Charlotte Brontë! She has not been as other women, protected by the grave from all betrayal of the esipodes in her own life. Everybody has betrayed her, and all she thought about this one and that, and every name that was ever associated with hers. There was a Mr. Taylor from London about whom she wrote with great freedom to her friend Miss Nussey, telling how the little man had come, how he had gone away without any advance in the affairs, how a chill came over her when he appeared and she found him much less attractive than when at a distance, yet how she liked it as little when he went away and was somewhat excited about his first letter, and even went so far as to imagine with a laugh that there might be possibly a dozen little Joe Taylors before all was over. She was hard upon Miss Austen for having no comprehension of passion, but no one could have been cooler and less impassioned than she as she considered the question of Mr. Taylor, reluctant to come to any decision yet disappointed when it came to nothing. There was no longing in her mind for Mr. Taylor, but there was for life and action and the larger paths and the little Joes.

This longing which she expressed with so much vehemence and some poetic fervour as the burden of the lives of Shirley and her friends has been the keynote of a great deal that has followed—the revolts and

By MRS. OLIPHANT

rebellions, the wild notions about marriage, the "Sex Problem," and a great deal more. From that first point to the prevailing discussion of all the questions involved is a long way; but it is a matter of logical progression, and when once the primary matter is opened, every enlargement of the subject may be taken as a thing to be expected. Charlotte Brontë was in herself the embodiment of all old-fashioned restrictions. She was proper, she was prim, her life was hedged in by all the little rules which bind the primitive woman. But when she left her little recluse behind and rushed into the world of imagination her exposure of the bondage in which she sat with all her sisters was far more daring than if she had been a woman of many experiences and knew what she was speaking of. She did know the longing, the discontent, the universal contradiction and contrariety which is involved in that condition of unfulfilment to which so many grey and undeveloped lives are condemned. For her and her class, which did not speak of it, everything depended upon whether the woman married or did not marry. Their thoughts were thus artificially fixed to one point in the horizon, but their ambition was neither ignoble nor unclean. It was bold, indeed, in proportion to its almost ridiculous innocence, and want of perception of any grosser side. Their share in life, their part in the mutual building of the house, was what they sought. But the seed she thus sowed has come to many growths which would have appalled Charlotte Brontë. Those who took their first inspiration from this cry of hers, have quite forgotten what it was she wanted, which was not emancipation but an extended duty. But while it would be very unjust to blame her for the vagaries that have followed and to which nothing could be less desirable than any building of the house or growth of the race, any responsibility or service—we must still believe that it was she who drew the curtain first aside and opened the gates to imps of evil meaning, polluting and profaning the domestic hearth.

The marriage which—after all these wild embodiments of the longing and solitary heart which could not consent to abandon its share in life, after Shirley and Lucy Snowe, and that complex unity of three female souls all unfulfilled, which had now been broken by death—she accepted in the end of her life, is the strangest commentary upon all that went before, or rather, upon all the literary and spiritual part of her history, though it was a quite appropriate ending to Mr. Brontë's daughter, and even to the writer of those sober letters which discussed Mr. Taylor, whether he should or should not be encouraged, and how it was a little disappointing after all to see him go away. Her final suitor was one of the class which she had criticised so scathingly, one who, it might have been thought, would scarcely have ventured to enter the presence or brave the glance of so penetrating an eye, but who would seem to have brought all the urgency of a *grand passion* to the sombre parlour of the parsonage, to the afternoon stillness of the lonely woman who would not seem to have suspected anything of the kind till it was poured out before her without warning. She was startled and confused by his declaration and appeal, never apparently having contemplated the possibility of any such occurrence; and in the interval which followed the father raged and resisted, and the lover did not conceal his heartbroken condition but suffered without complaining while the lady looked on wistful, touched and attracted by the unlooked-for love, and gradually melting towards that, though indifferent to the man who offered it. Mr. Brontë evidently thought that if this now distinguished daughter who had been worshipped among the great people in London, and talked of in all the newspapers, married at all in her mature age, it should be some one distinguished like herself, and not the mere curate who was the natural fate of every clergyman's daughter, the simplest and least known.

Charlotte meanwhile said no word, but saw the curate enact various tragic follies of love for her sake with a sort of awe and wonder, astonished to find herself thus possessed still of the charm which none are so sure as women that only youth and beauty can be expected to possess. And she had never had any beauty, and, though she was not old, was no longer young. It is a conventional fiction that a woman still in the thirties is beyond the exercise of that power. Indeed, it would be hard to fix the age at which the spell departs. Certainly the demeanour of Mr. Nicholls gave her full reason to believe that it had not departed from her. He faltered in the midst of the service, grew pale, almost lost his self-possession when he suddenly saw her among the kneeling figures round the altar ; and no doubt this rather shocking and startling exhibition of his feelings was more pardonable to the object of so much emotion than it was likely to have been to any other spectator. The romance is a little strange, but yet it is a romance in its quaint ecclesiastical way. And soon Charlotte was drawn still more upon her lover's side by the violence of her father. It was decided that the curate was to go, and that this late gleam of love-making was to be extinguished and the old dim atmosphere to settle down again for ever. Finally, however, the mere love of love, which had always been more to her than any personal inclination, and the horror of that permanent return to the twilight of dreamy living against which she had struggled all her life, overcame her, and gave her courage ; but she married characteristically, not as women marry who are carried to a new home and make a new beginning in life, but retaining all the circumstances of the old and receiving her husband into her father's house where she had already passed through so many fluctuations and dreamed so many dreams, and which was full to overflowing with the associations of the past.

We have no reason to suppose that it did not add to the happiness of her life ; indeed, every indication is to the contrary, and the husband seems to have been kind, considerate and affectionate. Still this thing upon which so many of her thoughts had been fixed during her whole life, which she had felt to be the necessary condition of full development, and for which the little impassioned female circle of which she was the expositor had sighed and cried to heaven and earth, came to her at last very much in the form of a catastrophe. No doubt the circumstances of her quickly failing health and shortened life promote this feeling. But without really taking these into consideration the sensation remains the same. The strange little keen soul with its sharply fixed restrictions, yet intense force of perception within its limits, dropped out of the world into which it had made an irruption so brilliant and so brief and sank out of sight altogether, sank into the humdrum house between the old father and the sober husband, into the clerical atmosphere with which she had no sympathy, into the absolute quiet of domestic life to which no Prince Charming could now come gaily round the corner, out of the mists and moors, and change with a touch of his wand the grey mornings and evenings into golden days. Well! was not this that which she had longed for, the natural end of life towards which her Shirley, her Caroline, her Lucy had angrily stretched forth their hands, indignant to be kept waiting, clamouring for instant entrance? And so it was, but how different! Lucy Snowe's little housekeeping, all the preparations which M. Paul made for her comfort and which seemed better to her than any palace, would not they too have taken the colour of perpetual dulness if everything had settled down and the Professor assumed his slippers by the domestic hearth? Ah no, for Lucy Snowe loved the man, and Charlotte Brontë, as appears, loved only the love. It is a parable. She said a little later that she began to see that this was the fate which she would wish for those she loved best, for her friend Ellen, perhaps for her Emily if she had lived—the good

By MRS. OLIPHANT

man very faithful, very steady, worth his weight in gold —yet flatter than the flattest days of old, *solidement nourri*, a good substantial husband, managing all the parish business, full of talk about the Archdeacon's charge, and the diocesan meetings, and the other clergy of the moorland parishes. We can conceive that she got to fetching his slippers for him and taking great care that he was comfortable, and perhaps had it been so ordained might have grown into a contented matron and forgotten the glories and miseries, so inseparably twined and linked together, of her youth. But she only had a year in which to do all that, and this is how her marriage seems to turn into a catastrophe, the caging of a wild creature that had never borne captivity before, and which now could no longer rush forth into the heart of any shining *fête*, or to the window of a strange confessional, anywhere, to throw off the burden of the perennial contradiction, the ceaseless unrest of the soul, the boilings of the volcano under the snow.

I have said it was difficult to account for the extreme interest still attaching to everything connected with Charlotte Brontë; not only the story of her peculiar genius, but also of everybody connected with her, though the circle was in reality quite a respectable, humdrum, and uninteresting one, containing nobody of any importance except the sister, who was her own wilder and fiercer part. One way, however, in which these sisters have won some part of their long-lasting interest is due to the treatment to which they have been subjected. They are the first victims of that ruthless art of biography which is one of the features of our time; and that not only by Mrs. Gaskell, who took up her work in something of an apologetic vein, and was so anxious to explain how it was that her heroine expressed certain ideas not usual in the mouths of women, that she was compelled to take away the reputation of a number of other people in order to excuse the peculiarities of these two remarkable women. But everybody who has touched their history since, and there have been many—for it would seem that gossip, when restrained by no bonds of decorum or human feeling, possesses a certain interest whether it is concerned with the household of a cardinal or that of a parish priest—has followed the same vicious way without any remonstrance or appeal for mercy. We have all taken it for granted that no mercy was to be shown to the Brontës. Let every rag be torn from Charlotte, of whom there is the most to say. Emily had the good luck to be no correspondent, and so has escaped to some degree the complete exposure of every confidence and every thought which has happened to her sister. Is it because she has nobody to defend her that she has been treated thus barbarously? I cannot conceive a situation more painful, more lacerating to every feeling, than that of the father and the husband dwelling silent together in that sombre parsonage, from which every ray of light seems to depart with the lost woman, whose presence had kept a little savour in life, and looking on in silence to see their life taken to pieces, and every decent veil dragged from the inner being of their dearest and nearest. They complained as much as two voiceless persons could, or at least the father complained: and the very servants came hot from their kitchen to demand a vindication of their character: but nobody noted the protest of the old man amid the silence of the moors: and the husband was more patient and spoke no word. Even he, however, after nearly half a century, when that far-off episode of life must have become dim to him, has thrown his relics open for a little more revelation, a little more interference with the helpless ashes of the dead.

No dot is now omitted upon i, no t left uncrossed. We know, or at least are told, who Charlotte meant by every character she ever portrayed, even while the model still lives. We know her opinion of her friends, or rather acquaint-

THE SISTERS BRONTË

ances, the people whom she saw cursorily and formed a hasty judgment upon, as we all do in the supposed safety of common life. Protests have been offered in other places against a similar treatment of other persons; but scarcely any protest has been attempted in respect to Charlotte Brontë. The resurrection people have been permitted to make their researches as they pleased. It throws a curious pathos, a not unsuitably tragic light upon a life always so solitary, that this should all have passed in silence because there was actually no one to interfere, no one to put a ban upon the dusty heaps and demand that no more should be said. When one looks into the matter a little more closely, one finds it is so with almost all those who have specially suffered at the hands of the biographer. The Carlyles had no child, no brother to rise up in their defence. It gives the last touch of melancholy to the conclusion of a lonely life. Mrs. Gaskell, wise woman, defended herself from a similar treatment by will, and left children behind her to protect her memory. But the Brontës are at the mercy of every one who cares to give another raking to the diminished heap of *débris*. The last writer who has done so, Mr. Clement Shorter, had some real new light to throw upon a story which surely has now been sufficiently turned inside out, and has done his work with

By MRS. OLIPHANT

perfect good feeling, and, curiously enough after so many exploitations, in a way which shows that interest has not yet departed from the subject. But we trust that now the memory of Charlotte Brontë will be allowed to rest.

Mrs. W. Oliphant

GEORGE ELIOT

By MRS. LYNN LINTON

GEORGE ELIOT

IN this essay it is not intended to go into the vexed question of George Eliot's private life and character. Death has resolved her individuality into nothingness, and the discrepancy between her lofty thoughts and doubtful action no longer troubles us. But her work still remains as common property for all men to appraise at its true value—to admire for its beauty, to reverence for its teaching, to honour for its grandeur, yet at the same time to determine its weaknesses and to confess where it falls short of the absolute perfection claimed for it in her lifetime.

For that matter indeed, no one has suffered from unmeasured adulation more than has George Eliot. As a philosopher, once bracketed with Plato and Kant; as a novelist, ranked the highest the world has seen; as a woman, set above the law and, while living in open and admired adultery, visited by bishops and judges as well as by the best of the laity ; her faults of style and method praised as genius —since her death she has been treated with some of that reactionary neglect which always follows on extravagant esteem. The mud-born ephemeridæ of literature have dispossessed her. For her profound learning, which ran like a golden thread through all she wrote till it became tarnished by pedantry, we have the ignorance which misquotes Lemprière and thinks itself classic. For her outspoken language and forcible diction, wherein, however, she always preserved so much modesty, and for her realism which described things and feelings as they are, but without going into revolting details, we have those lusciously suggestive epithets and those unveiled presentations of the sexual instinct which seem to make the world one large lupanar. For her accurate science and profound philosophy, we have those claptrap phrases which have passed into common speech and are glibly reproduced by facile parrots who do not understand and never could have created ; and for her scholarly diction we have the tawdriness of a verbal ragbag where grammar is as defective as taste. Yet our modern tinselled dunces have taken the place of the one who, in her lifetime, was made almost oppressively great—almost too colossal in her supremacy.

But when all this rubbish has been thrown into the abyss

of oblivion, George Eliot's works will remain solid and alive, together with Thackeray's, Scott's and Fielding's. Our Immortals will include in their company, as one of the "choir invisible" whose voice will never be stilled for man, the author of "Adam Bede" and "Romola," of the "Mill on the Floss" and "Middlemarch."

Her first essays in fiction, her "Scenes of Clerical Life," show the germs of her future greatness as well as the persistency of her aim. In "Janet's Repentance," which to our mind is the best of the three, those germs are already shaped to beauty. Nothing can be more delicately touched than the nascent love between Janet and Mr. Tryon. No more subtle sign of Janet's besetting sin could be given than by that candlestick held "aslant;" while her character, compounded of pride, timidity, affectionateness, spiritual aspiration and moral degradation, is as true to life as it was difficult to portray. It would be impossible to note all the gems in these three stories. We can indicate only one or two. That splendid paragraph in "Mr. Gilfil's Love Story," beginning: "While this poor heart was being bruised"—the sharp summing up of Mr. Amos Barton's "middling" character —Lady Cheverel's silent criticisms contrasted with her husband's iridescent optimism—the almost Shakesperean humour of the men, the author's keen appraisement of the commonplace women ; such aphorisms as Mrs. Linnet's "It's right enough to be speritial—I'm no enemy to that—but I like my potatoes meally ; "—these and a thousand more, eloquent, tender, witty, deep, make these three stories masterpieces in their way, despite the improbability of the Czerlaski episode in "Amos Barton" and the inherent weakness of the Gilfil plot. We, who can remember the enthusiasm they excited when they first appeared in *Blackwood's Magazine*, on re-reading them in cooler blood can understand that enthusiasm, though we no longer share its pristine intensity. It was emphatically a new departure in literature, and the noble note of that religious feeling which is independent of creed and which touches all hearts alike, woke an echo that even to this day reverberates though in but a poor, feeble and attenuated manner.

"Adam Bede," the first novel proper of the long series, shows George Eliot at her best in her three most noteworthy qualities—lofty principles, lifelike delineation of character, and fine humour, both broad and subtle. The faults of the story are the all-pervading anachronism of thought and circumstance ; the dragging of the plot in the earlier half of the book ; and the occasional ugliness of style, where, as in that futile opening sentence the author as I directly addresses the reader as You. The scene is laid in the year 1799—before the Trades Unions had fixed a man's hours of work so accurately as to make him leave off with a screw half driven in, so soon as the clock begins to strike—before too the hour of leaving off was fixed at six. We older people can remember when workmen wrought up to eight and were never too exact even then. Precision of the kind practised at the present day was not known then; and why were there no apprentices in Adam's shop? Apprentices were a salient feature in all the working community, and no shop could have existed without them. Nor would the seduction by the young squire of a farmer's niece or daughter have been the heinous crime George Eliot has made it. If women of the lower class held a somewhat better position than they did in King Arthur's time, when, to be the mother of a knight's bastard, raised a churl's wife or daughter far above her compeers and was assumed to honour not degrade her, they still retained some of the old sense of inferiority. Does any one remember that famous answer in the Yelverton trial not much more than a generation ago? In 1799 Hetty's mishap would have been condoned by all concerned, save perhaps by Adam himself; and Arthur Donnithorne would have suffered no more for his escapade than did our well-known Tom Jones for his little diversions. And—

were there any night schools for illiterate men in 1799 ? And how was that reprieve got so quickly at a time when there were neither railroads nor telegraphs ?—indeed, would it have been got at all in days when concealment of birth alone was felony and felony was death ? Also, would Hetty have been alone in her cell ? In 1799 all prisoners were herded together, young and old, untried and condemned ; and the separate system was not in existence. Save for Hetty's weary journey on foot and in chance carts, the story might have been made as of present time with more *vraisemblance* and harmoniousness.

These objections apart, how supreme the whole book is ! The characters stand out fresh, firm and living. As in some paintings you feel as if you could put your hand round the body, so in George Eliot's writings you feel that you have met those people in the flesh, and talked to them, holding them by the hand and looking into their eyes. There is not a line of loose drawing anywhere. From the four Bedes, with that inverted kind of heredity which Zola has so powerfully shown, to the stately egoism of Mrs. Irwine— from the marvellous portraiture of Hetty Sorrel with her soft, caressing, lusciously-loving outside, and her heart " as hard as a cherry-stone " according to Mrs. Poyser— from the weak-willed yet not conscienceless Arthur Donnithorne to the exquisite purity of Dinah, the character-drawing is simply perfect. Many were people personally known to George Eliot, and those who were at all behind the scenes recognised the portraits. Down at Wirksworth they knew the Bedes, Dinah, the Poysers, and some others. In London, among the intimates of George Lewes, Hetty needed no label. Mrs. Poyser's good things were common property in the neighbourhood long before George Eliot crystallised them for all time, and embellished them by her matchless setting; and Dinah's sermon was not all imaginary. But though in some sense her work was portraiture, it was portraiture passed through the alembic of her brilliant genius, from commonplace material distilled into the finest essence.

It is impossible here again to give adequate extracts of the wise, witty, tender and high-minded things scattered broadcast over this book—as, indeed, over all that George Eliot ever wrote. That paragraph beginning—"Family likeness has often a deep sadness in it"; the description of Hetty's flower-like beauty, which fascinated even her sharp-tongued aunt; phrases like "John considered a young master as the natural enemy of an old servant," and "young people in general as a poor contrivance for carrying on the world"; that sharp little bit of moral and intellectual antithesis, with the learned man "meekly rocking the twins in the cradle with his left hand, while with his right he inflicted the most lacerating sarcasms on an opponent who had betrayed a brutal ignorance of Hebrew"—forgiving human weaknesses and moral errors as is a Christian's bounden duty, but treating as "the enemy of his race, the man who takes the wrong side on the momentous subject of the Hebrew points"; how masterly, how fine are these and a dozen other unnoted passages!

Hetty in her bedroom, parading in her concealed finery, reminds one too closely of Gretchen with her fatal jewels to be quite favourable to the English version; and we question the truth of Adam Bede's hypothetical content with such a Dorothy Doolittle as his wife. Writers of love stories among the working classes in bygone days forget that notableness was then part of of a woman's virtue—part of her claims to love and consideration—and that mere flower-like kittenish prettiness did not count to her honour any more than graceful movements and æsthetic taste would count to the honour of a Tommy in the trenches who could neither handle a spade nor load a rifle. Blackmore made the same mistake in his "Lorna Doone," and George Eliot has repeated it in Adam's love for Hetty solely for her beauty and without "faculty" as her dower. In his own way Bartle Massey, misogynist, is as smart as Mrs. Poyser herself, as amusing and as trenchant ; but the coming-of-age dance is fifty years and more too modern, and the long dissertation at the beginning of the second book is a blot, because it is a clog and an interruption. Not so that glorious description of nature in August when "the sun was hidden for a moment and then shone out warm again like a recovered joy ; "—nor that deep and tender bit of introspection, setting forth the spiritual good got from sorrow as well as its indestructible impress.

Yet for all the beauty of these philosophic passages there are too many of them in this as in all George Eliot's works. They hamper the action and lend an air of pedantry and preaching with which a novel proper has nothing to do. It is bad style as well as bad art, and irritating to a critical, while depressing to a sympathetic reader. But summing up all the faults together, and giving full weight to each, we gladly own the masterly residuum that is left. The dawning love between Adam and Dinah alone is enough to claim for "Adam Bede" one of the highest places in literature, had not that place been already taken by the marvellous truth, diversity and power of the character-drawing. Mrs. Poyser's epigrams, too, generally made when she was "knitting with fierce rapidity, as if her movements were a necessary function like the twittering of a crab's antennæ," both too numerous

GEORGE ELIOT

and too well known to quote, would have redeemed the flimsiest framework and the silliest padding extant.

The light that seemed to flash on the world when this glorious book was published will never be forgotten by those who were old enough at the time to read and appreciate. By the way, is that would-be famous Liggins still alive? When he sums it all up, how much did he get out of his bold attempt to don the giant's robe?

If "Adam Bede" was partly reminiscent, "The Mill on the Floss" was partly autobiographical. There is no question that in the sensitive, turbulent, loving nature of Maggie Tulliver Marian Evans painted herself. Those who knew her when she first came to London knew her as a pronounced insurgent. Never noisy and never coarse, always quiet in manner, sensitive, diffident and shrinking from unpleasantness, she yet had not put on that "made" and artificial pose which was her distinguishing characteristic in later years. She was still Maggie Tulliver, with a conscience and temperament at war together, and with a spiritual ideal in no way attained by her practical realisation. For indeed, the union between Marian Evans and George Lewes was far more incongruous in some of its details than was Maggie's love for Philip or her passion for Stephen. Philip appealed to her affection of old time, her pity and her love of art—Stephen to her hot blood and her sensuous love of beauty. But George Lewes's total want of all religiousness of feeling, his brilliancy of wit, which was now coarse now mere *persiflage*, his cleverness, which was more quickness of assimilation than the originality of genius, were all traits of character unlike the deeper, truer and more ponderous qualities of the woman who braved the world for his sake when first she linked her fate with his—the woman who did not, like Maggie, turn back when she came to the brink but who boldly crossed the Rubicon—and who, in her after efforts to cover up the conditions, showed that she smarted from the consequences.

Read in youth by the light of sympathy with insurgency, Maggie is adorable, and her brother Tom is but a better-looking Jonas Chuzzlewit. Read in age by the light of respect for conformity and self-control, much of Maggie's charm vanishes, while most of Tom's hardness becomes both respectable and inevitable. Maggie was truly a thorn in the side of a proud country family, not accustomed to its little daughters running off to join the gipsies, nor to its grown girls eloping with their cousin's lover. Tom was right when he said no reliance could be placed on her; for where there is this unlucky divergence between principle and temperament, the will can never be firm nor the walk steady. Sweet little Lucy had more of the true heroism of a woman in her patient acceptance of sorrow and her generous forgiveness of the cause thereof, than could be found in all Maggie's struggles between passion and principle. The great duties of life lying at our feet and about our path cannot be done away with by the romantic picturesqueness of one character contrasted with the more prosaic because conventional limitations of the other; nor is it right to give all our sympathy to the one who spoilt so many lives and brought so much disgrace on her family name, merely because she did not mean, and did not wish, and had bitter remorse after terrible conflicts, which never ended in real self-control or steadfast pursuance of the right.

There is something in "The Mill on the Floss" akin to the gloomy fatalism of a Greek tragedy. In "Adam Bede" is more spontaneity of action, more liberty of choice; but, given the natures by which events were worked out to their final issues in "The Mill on the Floss," it seems as if everything must have happened precisely as it did. An obstinate, litigious and irascible man like Mr. Tulliver was bound to come to grief in the end. Fighting against long odds as he did, he could not win. Blind anger and as blind precipitancy, against cool tenacity and clear perceptions, must go under; and Mr. Tulliver was no match against the laws of life as interpreted by Mr. Wakem and the decisions of the law courts. His choice of a fool for his wife—was not Mrs. Tulliver well known at Coventry?—was another step in the terrible March of Fate. She was of no help to him as a wife—with woman's wit to assist his masculine decisions—nor as a mother was she capable of ruling her daughter or influencing her son. She was as a passive instrument in the hands of the gods—one of those unnoted and unsuspected agents by whose unconscious action such tremendous results are produced. George Eliot never did anything more remarkable than in the union she makes in this book between the most commonplace characters and the most majestic conception of tragic fate. There is not a stage hero among them all—not a pair of buskins for the whole company; but the conception is Æschylean, though the stage is no bigger than a doll's house.

The humour in "The Mill on the Floss" is almost as rich as that of "Adam Bede," though the special qualities of the four sisters are perhaps unduly exaggerated. Sister Pullet's eternal tears become wearisome, and lose their effect by causeless and ceaseless repetition; and surely sister Grigg could not have been always such an unmitigated Gorgon! Mrs. Tulliver's helpless foolishness and tactless interference, moving with her soft white hands the lever which set the whole crushing machinery in motion, are after George Eliot's best manner; and the whole comedy circling round sister Pullet's wonderful bonnet and the linen and the chaney—comedy at last linked on to tragedy—is of inimitable richness. The girlish bond of sympathy between sister Pullet and sister Tulliver, in that they both liked spots for their patterned linen, while sister Grigg—allays contrairy to Sophy Pullet, would have striped things—is repeated in that serio-comic scene of the ruin, when the Tullivers are sold up and the stalwart cause of their disaster is in bed, paralysed. By the way, would he have recovered so quickly and so thoroughly as he did from such a severe attack? Setting that aside, for novelists are not expected to be very accurate pathologists, the humour of this part of the book is all the more striking for the pathos mingled with it.

"The head miller, a tall broad-shouldered man of forty, black-eyed and black-haired, subdued by a general mealiness like an auricula":—"They're nash things, them lop-eared rabbits—they'd happen ha' died if they'd been fed. Things out o' natur never thrive. God Almighty doesn't like 'em. He made the rabbit's ears to lie back, and it's nothing but contrariness to make 'em lie down like a mastiff dog's":—"Maggie's tears began to subside, and she put out her mouth for the cake and bit a piece; and then Tom bit a piece, just for company, and they ate together and rubbed each other's cheeks and brows and noses together, while they ate, with a humiliating resemblance to two friendly ponies":—Is there anything better than these in Mrs. Poyser's repertory?

Of acute psychological vision is that fine bit on "plotting contrivance and deliberate covetousness"; and the summing up of the religious and moral life of the Dodsons and Tullivers, beginning " Certainly the religious and moral ideas of the Dodsons and Tullivers," is as good as anything in our language. No one theoretically knew human nature better than George Eliot. Practically, she was too thin-skinned to bear the slightest abrasion, such as necessarily comes to us from extended intercourse or the give and take of equality. But theoretically she sounded the depths and shallows, and knew where the bitter springs rose and where the healing waters flowed; and when she translated what she knew into the conduct and analysis of her fictitious characters, she gave them a life and substance peculiarly her own.

Hitherto George Eliot has dealt with her own experiences, her reminiscences of old friends and well-known places, of familiar acquaintances, and, in Maggie Tulliver, of her own childish frowardness and affectionateness—her girlish desire to do right and facile slipping into wrong. In "Silas Marner" she ventures into a more completely creative region; and, for all the exquisite beauty and poetry of the central idea, she has failed her former excellence. The story is one of the not quite impossible but highly improbable kind, with a *Deus ex machinâ* as the ultimate setter-to-rights of all things wrong. As with "Adam Bede," the date is thrown back a generation or two, without the smallest savour of the time indicated, save in the fashion of the dresses of the sisters Lammeter —a joseph substituted for a cloak, and riding on a pillion for a drive in a fly. Else there is not the least attempt to synchronise time, circumstances and sentiment, while the story is artificial in its plot and unlikely in its treatment. Yet it is both pretty and pathetic; and the little introduction of fairyland in the golden-haired child asleep by the fire, as the substitute for the stolen hoard, is as lovely as fairy stories generally are. But we altogether question the probability of a marriage between the young squire and his drunken wife. Such a woman would not have been too rigorous, and was not; and such a man as Godfrey Cass would not have married a low-born mistress from "a movement of compunction." As we said before, in the story of Hetty and Arthur, young squires a century ago were not so tender-hearted towards the honour of a peasant girl. It was a pity, of course, when things went wrong; but then young men will be young men, and it behoved the lasses to keep themselves to themselves! If the young squire did the handsome thing in money, that was all that could be expected of him. The girl would be none the worse thought of for her slip; and the money got by her fault would help in her plenishing with some honest fellow who understood things. This is the sentiment still to be found in villages, where the love-children of the daughters out in service are to be found comfortably housed in the grandmother's cottage, and where no one thinks any the worse of the unmarried mother; and certainly, a century ago, it was the universal rule of moral measurement. George Eliot undoubtedly made a chronological mistake in both stories by the amount of conscientious remorse felt by her young men, and the depth of social degradation implied in this slip of her young women.

The beginning of "Silas Marner" is much finer than that of either of her former books. It strikes the true note of a harmonious introduction, and is free from the irritating trivialities of the former openings. In those early days of which "Silas Marner" treats, a man from the next parish was held as a "stranger"; and even now a Scotch, Irish or Welsh man would be considered as much a foreigner as a "Frenchy" himself, were he to take up his abode in any of the more remote hamlets of the north or west. The state of isolation in which Silas Marner lived was true on all these counts—his being a "foreigner" to the autochthonous shepherds and farmers of Ravaloe—his half mazed, half broken-hearted state owing to the false accusation brought against him and the criminal neglect of Providence to show his innocence—and his strange and uncongenial trade. Yet, for this last, were not the women of that time familiar with the weaving industry?—else what could they have done with the thread which they themselves had spun? If it were disposed of to a travelling agent for the hand-loom weavers, why not have indicated the fact? It would have been one touch more to the good of local colour and conditional accuracy. To be sure, the paints are laid on rather thickly throughout; but eccentricities and folks with bees in their bonnets were always to be found in remote places before the broom of steam and electricity came to sweep them into a more common conformity; and that line between oddity and insanity, always narrow, was then almost invisible.

The loss of the hoarded treasure and the poor dazed weaver's terrified flight to the Rainbow introduces us to one of George Eliot's most masterly of her many scenes of rustic humour.

"The more important customers, who drank spirits and sat nearest the fire, staring at each other as if a bet were depending on the first man who winked; while the beer drinkers, chiefly men in fustian jackets and smock-frocks, kept their eyelids down and rubbed their hands across their mouths, as if their draughts of beer were a funereal duty attended with embarrassing sadness"—these, as well as Mr. Snell, the landlord, "a man of a neutral disposition, accustomed to stand aloof from human differences, as those of beings who were all alike in need of liquor"—do their fooling admirably. From the cautious discussion on the red Durham with a star on her forehead, to the authoritative dictum of Mr. Macey, tailor and parish clerk (were men of his social stamp called *Mr.* in those days?) when he asserts that "there's allays two 'pinions; there's the 'pinion a man has of himsen, and there's the 'pinion other folks have on him. There'd be two 'pinions about a cracked bell, if the bell could hear itself"—from the gossip about the Lammeter land to the ghos'es in the Lammeter stables, it is all excellent—rich, racy and to the manner born. And the sudden appearance of poor, scared, weazen-faced Silas in the midst of the discussion on ghos'es, gives occasion for another fytte of humour quite as good as what has gone before.

Worthy of Mrs. Poyser, too, was sweet and patient Dolly Winthrop's estimate of men. "It seemed surprising that Ben Winthrop, who loved his quart-pot and his joke, got along so well with Dolly; but she took her husband's jokes and joviality as patiently as everything else, considering that 'men *would* be so' and viewing the stronger sex in the light of animals whom it had pleased Heaven to make naturally troublesome, like bulls and turkey-cocks." Good, too, when speaking of his wife, is Mr. Macey's version of the "mum" and "budget" of the fairies' dance. "Before I said 'sniff' I took care to know as she'd say 'snaff,' and pretty quick too. I wasn't a-going to open *my* mouth like a dog at a fly, and snap it to again, wi' nothing to swaller."

But in spite of all this literary value of "Silas Marner" we come back to our first opinion of its being unreal and almost impossible in plot. The marriage of Godfrey to an opium-eating (?) drab, and the robbery of Silas Marner's hoard by the squire's son were pretty hard nuts to crack in the way of probability; but the timely death of the wife just at the right moment and in the right place—the adoption of a little girl of two by an old man as nearly "nesh" as was consistent with his power of living free from the restraint of care—the discovery of Dunsay's body and the restoration to the weaver of his long-lost gold—the *impasse* of Eppie, the squire's lawfully born daughter and his only legal inheritor, married to a peasant and living as a peasant at her father's gates: all these things make "Silas Marner" a beautiful unreality, taking it out of the ranks of human history and placing it in those of fairy tale and romance.

In "Felix Holt" we come back to a more actual kind of life, such as it was in the early thirties when the "democratic wave," which has swept away so much of the old parcelling out of things social and political, was first beginning to make itself felt. But here again George Eliot gives us the sense of anachronism in dealing too familiarly with those new conditions of the Reform Bill which gave Treby Magna for the first time a member, and which also for the first time created the Revising Barrister—while Trades Unions were still unrecognised by the law, and did their work mainly by rattening and violence. Any one who was an intelligent and wide-awake child at that time, and who can remember the talk of the excited elders, must remember things somewhat differently from what George Eliot has set down. Radical was in those days a term of reproach, carrying with it moral obloquy and condemnation. The Tories might call the Whigs Radicals when they wanted to overwhelm them with shame, as we might now say Anarchists and Dynamiters. But the most advanced Gentleman would never have stood for Parliament as a Radical. Felix Holt himself, and the upper fringe of the working class, as also the lower sediment, might be Radicals, but scarcely such a man as Harold Transome, who would have been a Whig of a broad pattern. And as for the Revising Barrister, he was looked on as something akin to Frankenstein's Monster. No one knew where his power began nor where it ended ; and on each side alike he was dreaded as an unknown piece of machinery which, once set a-going, no one could say what it would do or where it would stop.

In its construction "Felix Holt" is perhaps the most unsatisfactory of all George Eliot's books. The ins and outs of Transome and Durfey and Scaddon and Bycliffe were all too intricate in the weaving and too confused in the telling to be either intelligible or interesting. In trying on the garment of Miss Braddon the author of "Felix Holt" showed both want of perception and a deplorable misfit. Also she repeats the situation of Eppie and her adopted father Silas in that of Esther and Rufus Lyon. But where it was natural enough for the contentedly rustic Eppie to refuse to leave her beloved old father for one new and unknown—her old habits of cottage simplicity, including a suitable lover, for the unwelcome luxuries of an unfamiliar state—natural in her though eminently unnatural in the drama of life—it was altogether inharmonious with Esther's character and tastes to prefer poverty to luxury, Felix to Harold, Malhouse Yard to Transome Court. George Eliot's usually firm grip on character wavers into strange self-contradiction in her delineations of Esther Lyon. Even the situation of which she is so fond—the evolution of a soul from spiritual deadness to keen spiritual intensity, and the conversion of a mind from folly to seriousness—even in this we miss the masterly drawing of her better manner. The humour too is thinner. Mrs. Holt is a bad Mrs. Nickleby; and the comic chorus of rustic clowns, which George Eliot always introduces where she can, is comparatively poor. She is guilty of one distinct coarseness, in her own character as the author, when she speaks of the cook at Treby Manor—"a much grander person than her ladyship"—"as wearing gold and jewelry to a vast amount of suet."

When Esther has been taken up by the Transomes, George Eliot misses what would have been absolutely certain—these fine little points of difference between

GEORGE ELIOT

the high-bred lady of Transome Court and the half-bred Esther of Malhouse Yard ; and yet, quite unintentionally, she makes Esther as vulgar as a barmaid in her conversations and flirtatious coquetries with Harold Transome. Nor, we venture to think, as going too far on the other side, would a girl of Esther's upbringing and surroundings have used such a delightfully literary phrase as "importunate scents." On the whole we do not think it can be denied that, so far as she had gone in her literary career when she wrote "Felix Holt," it is undeniably her least successful work.

And yet, how many and how beautiful are the good things in it ! If Homer nods at times, when he is awake who can come near him ? The opening of the book is beyond measure fine, and abounds in felicitous phrases. " His sheep-dog following with heedless unofficial air as of a beadle in undress : "—" The higher pains of a dim political consciousness : "—" The younger farmers who had almost a sense of dissipation in talking to a man of his questionable station and unknown experience : "—" Her life would be exalted into something quite new—into a sort of difficult blessedness such as one may imagine in beings who are conscious of painfully growing into the possession of higher powers " (true for George Eliot herself but not for such a girl as Esther Lyon) :—These are instances of literary supremacy taken at random, with many more behind.

Then how exquisite is that first love-scene between Felix and Esther! It is in these grave and tender indications of love that George Eliot is at her best. Gentle as "sleeping flowers"—delicately wrought, like the most perfect cameos—graceful and suggestive, subtle and yet strong—they are always the very gems of her work. And in "Felix Holt" especially they stand out with more perfectness because of the inferior quality of so much that surrounds them.

Felix himself is one of George Eliot's masterpieces in the way of nobleness of ideal and firmness of drawing. Whether he would have won such a girl as Esther, or have allowed himself to be won by her, may be doubtful; but for all the rugged and disagreeable honesty of his nature—for all his high ideals of life and hideous taste in costume—for all his intrinsic tendency and external bearishness, he is supreme. And with one of George Eliot's best aphorisms, made in his intention, we close the book with that kind of mingled disappointment and delight which must needs be produced by the inferior work of a great master. "Blows are sarcasms turned stupid; wit is a form of force that leaves the limbs at rest."

GEORGE ELIOT

The last three books of the series are the most ponderous. Still beautiful and ever noble, they are like over-cultivated fruits and flowers of which the girth is inconvenient; and in one, at least, certain defects already discernible in the earlier issues attain a prominence fatal to perfect work.

Never spontaneous, as time went on George Eliot became painfully laboured. Her scholarship degenerated into pedantry, and what had been stately and dignified accuracy in her terms grew to be harsh and inartistic technicality. The artificial pose she had adopted in her life and bearing reacted on her work; and the contradiction between her social circumstances and literary position coloured more than her manners. All her teaching went to the side of self-sacrifice for the general good, of conformity with established moral standards, while her life was in direct opposition to her words; for though she did no other woman personal injustice, she did set an example of disobedience to the public law which wrought more mischief than was counteracted by even the noblest of her exhortations to submit to the restraints of righteousness, however irksome they might be. And it was this endeavour to co-ordinate insurgency and conformity, self-will and self-sacrifice, that made the discord of which every candid student of her work, who knew her history, was conscious from the beginning. Nowhere do we find this contradiction more markedly shown than in "Romola," the first of the ponderous last three.

Her noblest work, "Romola" is yet one of George Eliot's most defective in what we may call the scaffolding of the building. The loftiness of sentiment, the masterly delineation of character, the grand grasp of the political and religious movement of the time, the evidences of deep study and conscientious painstaking visible on every page, are combined with what seems to us to be the most extraordinary indifference to—for it cannot be ignorance of—the social and domestic conditions of the time. The whole story is surely impossible in view of the long arm of the Church—the personal restraints necessarily imposed on women during the turbulent unrest of the fifteenth and sixteenth centuries—the proud exclusiveness of the well-born citizens of any state.

Take the last first. Grant all the honour paid by Cosmo and Lorenzo to the learned men of all nations, especially to Greek scholars who, in the first fervour of the Renaissance, were as sons of the gods to those thirsting for the waters of the divine spring. Grant, too, the example set by Bartolommeo Scala, who had given his beautiful daughter Alessandra in marriage to the "soldier-poet" Marullo; was it likely that even an

GEORGE ELIOT

eccentric old scholar like the blind Bardo de' Bardi should have so unreservedly adopted a nameless Greek adventurer, flung up like a second Ulysses from the waves, unvouched for by any sponsor and unidentified by any document? We allow that Bardo might have taken Tito as his scribe and secretary, seeing that the Cennini had already employed him, waif and stray as he was; but that he should have consented to his daughter's marriage with this stranger, and that her more conservative and more suspicious godfather, Bernado del Nero, should have consented, even if reluctantly, was just about as likely as that an English country gentleman should allow his daughter to marry a handsome gipsy.

If we think for a moment of what citizenship meant in olden times, the improbability of the whole of Tito's career becomes still more striking. As, in Athens, the Sojourner never stood on the same plane with the autochthon, so in Rome the Peregrinus was ineligible for public office or the higher kind of marriage; and though the stricter part of the law was subsequently relaxed in favour of a wider civic hospitality, the sentiment of exclusiveness remained, and indeed does yet remain in Italy. It seems more than improbable that Tito, a Greek adventurer, should have been employed in any political service, save perhaps as a base kind of scout and unhonoured spy.

By MRS. LYNN LINTON

That he should ever have taken the position of an accredited public orator was so contrary to all the old traditions and habits of thought as to be of the same substance as a fairy tale.

The character of Bardo, too, is non-Italian; and his modes of life and thought were as impossible as are some other things to be hereafter spoken of. The Church had a long arm, as we said, and a firm grip; and while it blinked indulgently enough at certain aberrations, it demanded the show of conformity in essentials. Lorenzo was a pagan, but he died receiving the Sacraments. The Borgias were criminals, but their professions of faith were loud-voiced and in true earnest. Men might inveigh against the evil lives of the clergy and the excesses of monks and nuns, but they had to confess God and the Church; and their diatribes had to be carefully worded—as witness Rabelais—or a plea would certainly be found for the fire and faggot—as with Fra Dolcino and Savonarola. So with conformity to the usages of life which, then and now, are considered integral to morality. It could not have been possible for Bardo to bring up his daughter "aloof from the debasing influence" of her own sex, and in a household with only one old man for a servant. The times did not allow it; no more than we should allow it now in this freer day. This womanless home for an

Italian girl at any time, more especially in the Middle Ages, when even young wives were bound to have their companions and duennas, is a serious blot in workmanship. So, indeed, is the whole of Romola's life, being anachronism and simply nineteenth-century English from start to finish.

The things which both she and Tessa did, and were allowed to do, are on a par with "Gulliver's Travels" and "Peter Wilkins." It was as impossible for Tessa, a pretty young unmarried girl, contadina as she was, to come into Florence alone, as for a peasant child of three years old to be sent with a message on business into the City of London alone. To this day well-conducted women of any class do not wander about the streets of Italian cities unaccompanied; and maidenhood is, as it always was, sacredly and jealously guarded. Nor could Romola have gone out and come in at her desire, as she is allowed by the author. With streets filled by the turbulent factions of the Bianchi and Neri, always ready for a fight or for a love-adventure, what would have happened to, and been thought of, a beautiful young woman slipping about within the city and outside the gates at all hours of the day and night? She is said to be either quite alone (!), as when she goes to Tessa's house, or merely accompanied by Monna Brigida, as when she goes to the convent to see her dying brother—which also, by the way, was impossible—or attended, at a distance, by old Maso when she attempts her flight as a solitary nun. She would have lost name and state had she committed these eccentricities; and had she persisted in them, she would have been sent to a convent—that refuge for sorrow, that shelter from danger, that prison for contumacy—and her godfather would have been the first to consign her to what was then the only safe asylum for women. The scene she has with Tito before Nello's shop is ludicrously impossible—as is their English-like return home together, without retinue or lights, just like a man and wife of to-day when she has been to fetch him from the public-house, or, if she be of the better class, from his club. English, too, is Romola's sitting up for her husband in her queer womanless establishment, and opening the door to him when he comes home late at night. For the matter of that, indeed, Tito's solitary rambles are as much out of line with the time, and the circumstances of that time, as is Romola's strange daring. No man of any note whatever appeared alone in the streets when out on a midnight expedition, either to commit murder or break the seventh commandment. He took some one with him, friend or servant, armed; and to this day you will not find Italians willingly walk alone at night. The whole of this kind of life, if necessary for the story, is dead against truth and probability. So is Romola's flight, disguised as a nun. Splendid as is the scene between her and Savonarola, the *vraisemblance* is spoilt by this impossibility of condition. Nor could any woman of that time, brought up in a city, have felt a sense of freedom when fairly outside the walls by herself on a strange road, going to meet an unknown fate and bound to an unknown bourne. She would have felt as a purdah woman of India suddenly turned loose in the streets and environs of Delhi—as felt all those women whose evidence we read of in matters of crime and murder, when they came face to face with the desolation of unprotectedness. Modern women call it freedom, but in the Middle Ages such a feeling did not exist. All these things are anachronisms; as much so as if a novelist of the twentieth century, writing of English life in the eighteenth, should clothe his women in knickerbockers, mount them on bicycles, and turn them into the football field and cricket-ground.

These exceptions taken to the scaffolding of the book, we are free to admire its glorious nobility of sentiment, its lofty purpose, its perfection of character-drawing, and the dramatic power of its various scenes. Nothing can excel the power with which Tito's character is shown in its gradual slipping from simple selfishness to positive criminality. The whole action may be summed up in George Eliot's own words.

"When, the next morning, Tito put this determination into act, he had chosen his colour in the game, and had given an inevitable bent to his wishes. He had made it impossible that he should not from henceforth desire it to be the truth that his father was dead ; impossible that he should not be tempted to baseness rather than that the precise facts of his conduct should not remain for ever concealed. Under every guilty secret there is hidden a brood of guilty wishes, whose unwholesome infecting life is cherished by the darkness. The contaminating effect of deeds often lies less in the commission than in the consequent adjustment of our desires—the enlistment of our self-interest on the side of falsity ; as, on the other hand, the purifying influence of public confession springs from the fact that by it the hope in lies is for ever swept away, and the soul recovers its noble attitude of sincerity."

But, giving every weight to the natural weakness, sweetness and affectionateness, as well as to the latent falsity of Tito's character, we cannot accept the Tessa episode as true to life in general, while it is eminently untrue to Italian life, especially of those times. Tessa herself, too, is wearisome with her tears and her kisses, her blue eyes and baby face, so incessantly repeated and harped on. She is as nauseating as she is impossible; and the whole story from first to last is an ugly blot on the book.

In Romola and in Savonarola we touch the heights. The "tall lily" is an exquisite conception and is supreme in human loveliness. Her two interviews with Savonarola are superbly done, and the gradual crushing down of her proud self-will under the passionate fervour of the priest is beyond praise both for style and psychology. So, too, are the changes in the great preacher himself—the first, when his simple earnestness of belief in his mission degenerates into self-consciousness and personal assumption, as is the way with all reformers—the second, when he abandons his later attitude, and the dross is burnt away as the hour of trial comes on him, and the World no longer stands between God and his soul. The final scenes of the Frate's public life are powerfully wrought, with all George Eliot's mastery and eloquence and deep religious fervour; but it is in scenes and circumstances of this kind that she is ever at her best. In humour and psychologic insight she is greater than any English woman writer we have had; in aphorisms she is unrivalled; but in playfulness she is clumsy, and in catching the moral, intellectual and social tone of the times of which she writes, she is nowhere.

By MRS. LYNN LINTON

Contrast Romola's character and manner of life—above all those two thoroughly English letters of hers—with all that we know of Vittoria Colonna, the purest and noblest woman of her day—which was Romola's—and at once we see the difference between them—the difference wrought by four centuries—Vittoria being essentially a woman of the time, though a head and shoulders above the ruck ; while Romola is as essentially a product of the nineteenth century, In spite of the local colour—which, after all, is only a wash—given by the descriptions of pageants and processions, and by the history of which George Eliot so ably mastered the details, the whole book is nineteenth century, from Monna Brigida's characteristically English speech about Tessa's place in the house and the children's sweets, to Romola's as characteristically English attitude and hygienic objections—from a little maiden, without a caretaker, carrying eggs to Piero, to Romola's solitary visit to the studio and night perambulations about the city.

All these shortcomings notwithstanding, "Romola" will ever remain one of the noblest works of our noblest author ; and, after all, did not Shakespeare make Hector quote Aristotle, and show all his Greeks and Romans and outlandish nondescripts from countries unknown to himself, as nothing but sturdy Englishmen, such as lived and loved in the times of the great Eliza? Where we have so much to admire—nay, to venerate—we may let the smaller mistakes pass. Yet they must be spoken of by those who would be candid and not fulsome—just and not flattering. By the way, did George Eliot know that "Baldassare" is the name of one of the devils invoked to this day by Sicilian witches?

The longest of all the novels, "Middlemarch," is the most interesting in its characters, its isolated scenes, its moral meaning and philosophic extension; but it is also the most inartistic and the most encumbered with subordinate interests and personages. The canvas is as crowded as one of George Cruikshank's etchings; and the work would have gained by what George Eliot would have called fission—a division into two. The stories of Dorothea and Casaubon and of Rosamond and Lydgate are essentially separate entities; and though they are brought together at the last by an intermingled interest, the result is no more true unification than the Siamese twins or the Double-headed Nightingale represented one true human being. The contrast between the two beautiful young wives is well preserved, and the nicer shades of difference are as clearly marked as are the more essential; for George Eliot was far too good a workman to scamp in any direction, and the backs of her stories are as well wrought as the fronts. But if one-third of the book had been cut out—failing that fission, which would have been still better—the work would have gained in proportion to its compression.

The character of Dorothea marks the last stage in the development of the personality which begins with Maggie Tulliver, and is in reality Marian Evans's own self. Maggie, Romola and Dorothea are the same person in progressive stages of moral evolution. All are at cross corners with life and fate—all are rebellious against things as they find them. Maggie's state of insurgency is the crudest and simplest; Romola's is the most passionate in its moral reprobation of accepted unworthiness; Dorothea's is the widest in its mental horizon, and the most womanly in the whole-hearted indifference to aught but love, which ends the story and gives the conclusive echo. In its own way, her action in taking Will Ladislaw is like Esther's in marrying Felix Holt; but it has not the unlikelihood of Esther's choice. It is all for love, if one will, but it runs more harmoniously with the broad lines of her character, and gives us no sense of that dislocation which we get from Esther's decision. And in its own way it is at once a parallel and an apology.

The most masterly bits of work in " Middlemarch " are

the characters of Rosamond and Casaubon. Rosamond's unconscious selfishness, her moral thinness, and the superficial quality of her love are all portrayed without a flaw in the drawing; while Casaubon's dryness, his literary indecision following on his indefatigable research, and his total inability to adjust himself to his new conditions, together with his scrupulous formality of politeness combined with real cruelty of temper, make a picture of supreme psychologic merit. They who think that Casaubon was meant for the late Rector of Lincoln know nothing about George Eliot's early life. They who do know some of those obscurer details, are well aware of the origin whence she drew her masterly portrait, as they know who was Mrs. Poyser, who Tom Tulliver, and who Hetty Sorel. Hetty, indeed, is somewhat repeated in that amazingly idiotic Tessa, who is neither English nor Italian, nor, indeed, quite human in her molluscous silliness; but there are lines of relation which show themselves to experts, and the absence of the "cherry stone" does not count for more than the dissimilarity always to be found between two copies.

No finer bit of work was ever done than the deep and subtle but true and most pathetic tragedy of Lydgate's married life. The character of Rosamond was a difficult one to paint, and one false touch could have been fatal.

By MRS. LYNN LINTON

To show her intense selfishness and shallowness and yet not to make her revolting, was what only such a consummate psychologist as George Eliot could have done. And to show how Lydgate, strong man as he was and full of noble ambition and splendid aims, was necessarily subdued, mastered and ruined by the tenacious weakness and moral unworthiness of such a wife, yet not to make him contemptible, was also a task beyond the power of any but the few Masters of our literature. All the scenes between this ill-assorted pair are in George Eliot's best manner and up to her highest mark; and the gradual declination of Rosamond's love, together with Lydgate's gradual awakening to the truth of things as they were, are portrayed with a touch as firm as it is tender.

That scene on the receipt of Sir Godwin's letter is as tragic in its own way as Othello or a Greek drama. It has in it the same sense of human helplessness in the presence of an overmastering fate. Rosamond was Lydgate's Fate. Her weakness, tenacity and duplicity—his stronger manhood, which could not crush the weaker woman—his love, which could not coerce, nor punish, nor yet control the thing he loved—all made the threads of that terrible net in which he was entangled, and by which the whole worth of his life was destroyed. It is a story that

GEORGE ELIOT

goes home to the consciousness of many men, who know, as Lydgate knew, that they have been mastered by the one who to them is "as an animal of another and feebler species"—who know, as Lydgate knew, that their energies have been stunted, their ambition has been frustrated, and their horizon narrowed and darkened because of that tyranny which the weaker woman so well knows how to exercise over the stronger man.

Casaubon is as masterly in drawing as is Rosamond or Lydgate. We confess to a sadly imperfect sympathy with Dorothea in her queer enthusiasm for this dry stick of a man. Learned or not, he was scarcely one to whom a young woman, full of life's strong and sweet emotions, would care to give herself as a wife. One can understand the more impersonal impulse which threw Marian Evans into an attitude of adoration before the original of her dry stick; but when it comes to the question of marriage, the thing is simply revolting as done by the girl, not only of her own free-will but against the advice and prayers of her friends. Tom was to be excused for his harshness and irritation against Maggie; and Celia's commonplaces of wisdom for the benefit of that self-willed and recalcitrant Dodo, if not very profound nor very stimulating, nor yet sympathetic, were worth more in the daily life and ordering of sane folk than Dorothea's blind and obstinate determina-

By MRS. LYNN LINTON

tion. Beautiful and high-minded as she is, she is also one of those irritating saints whose virtues one cannot but revere, whose personal charms one loves and acknowledges, and whose wrongheadedness makes one long to punish them—or at least restrain them by main force from social suicide. And to think that to her first mistake she adds that second of marrying Will Ladislaw—the utter snob that he is! Where were George Eliot's perceptions? Or was it that in Ladislaw she had a model, near at hand, whom she saw through coloured glasses, which also shed their rosy light on her reproduction, so that her copy was to her as idealised as the original, and she was ignorant of the effect produced on the clear-sighted? Yet over all the mistakes made by her through defective taste and obstinate unwisdom, the beauty of Dorothea's character stands out as did Romola's—like a "white lily" in the garden. She is a superb creature in her own way, and her disillusionment is of the nature of a tragedy. But what could any woman expect from a man who could write such a love-letter as that of Mr. Casaubon's?

The canvas of "Middlemarch" is overcrowded, as we said; yet how good some of the characters are! The sturdy uprightness, tempered with such loving sweetness, of Cabel Garth; the commonplace negation of all great and all unworthy qualities of the Vincys—Celia and Sir James—Mr. Farebrother and Mr. and Mrs. Cadwallader—all are supreme. We confess we do not care much for the portraiture of Mr. Bulstrode and his spiteful delator Raffles—George Eliot is not good at melodrama; also the whole episode of Mr. Featherstone's illness, with his watching family and Mary Garth, too vividly recalls old Anthony Chuzzlewit and all that took place round his death-bed and about his will, to give a sense of truth or novelty. George Eliot's power did not lie in the same direction as that of Charles Dickens, and the contrast is not to her advantage. Great humorists as both were, their humour was essentially different, and will not bear comparison.

No book that George Eliot ever wrote is without its wise and pithy aphorisms, its brilliant flashes of wit, its innumerable good things. Space will not permit our quoting one-tenth part of the good things scattered about these fascinating pages. Celia's feeling, which she stifled in the depths of her heart, that "her sister was too religious for family comfort. Notions and scruples were like spilt needles, making one afraid of treading or sitting down, or even eating:"—(But, farther on, what an unnecessary bit of pedantry!—"In short, woman was a problem which, since Mr. Brooke's mind felt blank before it, could be hardly less complicated than the *revolutions of an irregular solid.*")—Mrs. Cadwallader's sense of birth, so that a "De Bracy reduced to take his dinner in a basin would have seemed to her an example of pathos worth exaggerating; and I fear his aristocratic vices would not have horrified her. But her feeling towards the vulgar rich was a sort of religious hatred: "—" Indeed, she (Mrs. Waule) herself was accustomed to think that entire freedom from the necessity of behaving agreeably was included in the Almighty's intentions about families: "—" Strangers, whether wrecked and clinging to a raft, or duly escorted and accompanied by portmanteaus, have always had a circumstantial fascination for the virgin mind, against which native merit has urged itself in vain: "—" Ladislaw, a sort of Burke with a leaven of Shelley: "—" But it is one thing to like defiance, and another thing to like its consequences "—an observation wrung out of her own disturbed and inharmonious experience:—" That controlled self-consciousness of manner which is the expensive substitute for simplicity: "—These are a few picked out at random, but the wealth that remains behind is but inadequately represented by stray nuggets.

Before we close the volume we would like to note the one redeeming little flash of human tenderness

GEORGE ELIOT

in Mr. Casaubon when he had received his death-warrant from Lydgate, and Dorothea waits for him to come up to bed. It is the only tender and spontaneous moment in his life as George Eliot has painted it, and its strangeness makes its pathos as well as its truth.

The last of the lengthy three, and the last novel she wrote, "Daniel Deronda" is the most wearisome, the least artistic, and the most unnatural of all George Eliot's books. Of course it has the masterly touch, and, for all its comparative inferiority, has also its supreme excellence. But in plot, treatment and character it is far below its predecessors. Some of the characters are strangely unnatural. Grandcourt, for instance, is more like the French caricature of an English milord than like a possible English gentleman depicted by a compatriot. Deronda himself is a prig of the first water; while Gwendolen is self-contradictory all through—like a tangled skein of which you cannot find the end, and therefore cannot bring it into order and intelligibility. Begun on apparently clear lines of self-will, pride, worldly ambition and personal self-indulgence—without either conscience or deep affections—self-contained and self-controlled—she wavers off into a condition of moral weakness, of vagrant impulses and humiliating self-abandonment for which nothing that went before has prepared us.

That she should ever have loved, or even fancied she loved, such a frozen fish as Grandcourt was impossible to a girl so full of energy as Gwendolen is shown to be. Clear in her desires of what she wanted, she would have accepted him, as she did, to escape from the hateful life to which else she would have been condemned. But she would have accepted him without even that amount of self-deception which is portrayed in the decisive interview. She knew his cruel secret, and she deliberately chose to ignore it. So far good. It is what she would have done. But where is the logic of making her "carry on" as she did when she received the diamonds on her wedding-day? It was a painful thing, sure enough, and the mad letter that came with them was disagreeable enough; but it could not have been the shock it is described, nor could it have made Gwendolen turn against her husband in such sudden hatred, seeing that she already knew the whole shameful story. These are faults in psychology; and the conduct of the plot is also imperfect. George Eliot's plots are always bad when she attempts intricacy, attaining instead confusion and unintelligibility; but surely nothing can be much sillier than the whole story of Deronda's birth and upbringing, nor can anything be more unnatural than the character and conduct of his mother. What English gentleman would have brought up a legitimately-born Jewish child under conditions which made the whole world believe him to be his own illegitimate son? And what young man, brought up in the belief that he was an English gentleman by birth—leaving out on which side of the blanket—would have rejoiced to find himself a Jew instead? The whole story is improbable and far-fetched; as also is Deronda's rescue of Mirah and her unquestioning adoption by the Meyricks. It is all distortion, and in no wise like real life; and some of the characters are as much twisted out of shape as is the story. Sir Hugo Mallinger and Mr. and Mrs. Gascoigne are the most natural of the whole gallery—the defect of exaggeration or caricature spoiling most of the others.

Of these others, Gwendolen herself is far and away the most unsatisfactory. Her sudden hatred of her husband is strained; so is her love for Deronda; so is her repentance for her constructive act of murder. That she should have failed to throw the rope to Grandcourt, drowning in the sea, was perhaps natural enough. That she should have felt such abject remorse and have betrayed herself in such humiliating unreserve to Deronda was not. All through the story her action with regard to Deronda is dead against the base lines of her character, and is compatible only with such an overwhelming amount of physical passion as does sometimes make women mad. We have no hint of this. On the contrary, all that Gwendolen says is founded on spiritual longing for spiritual improvement—spiritual direction with no hint of sexual impulse. Yet she acts as one overpowered by that impulse—throwing to the winds pride, reserve, womanly dignity and common sense. Esther was not harmonious with herself in her choice of Felix Holt over Harold Transome, but Esther was naturalness incarnate compared with Gwendolen as towards Daniel Deronda. And the evolution of Esther's soul, and the glimpse given of Rosamond's tardy sense of some kind of morality, difficult to be believed as each was, were easy sums in moral arithmetic contrasted with the birth and sudden growth of what had been Gwendolen's very rudimentary soul—springing into maturity in a moment, like a fully-armed Athene, without the need of the more gradual process. Add to all these defects, an amount of disquisition and mental dissection which impedes the story till it drags on as slowly as a heavily laden wain—add the fatal blunder of making long scenes which do not help on the action nor elucidate the plot, and the yet more fatal blunder of causeless pedantry, and we have to confess that our great master's last novel is also her worst. But then the one immediately preceding was incomparably her best.

We come now to the beauties of the work—to the inimitable force of some phrases—to the noble aim and meaning of the story—to the lofty spirit informing all those interrupting disquisitions, which are really interpolated moral essays, and must not be confounded with padding. Take this little shaft aimed at that *Græculus esuriens* Lush, that "half-caste among gentlemen" and the *âme damnée* of Grandcourt. "Lush's love of ease was well satisfied at present, and if his puddings were rolled towards him in the dust he took the inside bits and found them relishing." Again: "We sit up at night to read about Cakya-Mouni, Saint Francis and Oliver Cromwell, but whether we should be glad for any one at all like them to call on us the next morning, still more to reveal himself as a new relation, is quite another matter:"—" A man of refined pride shrinks from making a lover's approaches to a woman whose wealth or rank might make them appear presumptuous or low-motived ; but Deronda was finding a more delicate difficulty in a position which, superficially taken, was the reverse of that—though, to an ardent reverential love, the loved woman has always a kind of wealth which makes a man keenly susceptible about the aspect of his addresses." (We

By MRS. LYNN LINTON

extract this sentence as an instance of George Eliot's fine feeling and delicate perception expressed in her worst and clumsiest manner.) " A blush is no language, only a dubious flag-signal, which may mean either of two contradictions."

"Grandcourt held that the Jamaican negro was a beastly sort of baptist Caliban ; Deronda said he had always felt a little with Caliban, who naturally had his own point of view and could sing a good song ; " " Mrs. Davilow observed that her father had an estate in Barbadoes, but that she herself had never been in the West Indies ; Mrs. Torrington was sure she should never sleep in her bed if she lived among blacks ; her husband corrected her by saying that the blacks would be manageable enough if it were not for the half-breeds ; and Deronda remarked that the whites had to thank themselves for the half-breeds."

It is in such "polite pea-shooting" as this that George Eliot shows her inimitable humour—the quick give-and-take of her conversations being always in harmony with her characters. But, indeed, unsatisfactory as a novel though "Daniel Deronda" is, it is full of beauties of all kinds, from verbal wit to the grandly colossal sublimity of Mordecai, and Deronda's outburst of passionate desire to weld the scattered Jews into one nation of which he should be the heart and brain.

Whatever George Eliot did bears this impress of massive sincerity—of deep and earnest feeling—of lofty purpose and noble teaching. She was not a fine artist, and she spoilt her later work by pedantry and overlay, but she stands out as the finest woman writer we have had or probably shall have—stands a head and shoulders above the best of the rest. She touched the darker parts of life and passion, but she touched them with clean hands and a pure mind, and with that spirit of philosophic truth which *can* touch pitch and not be defiled. Yet prolific as she was, and the creator of more than one living character, she was not a flexible writer and her range was limited. She repeated situations and motives with a curious narrowness of scope, and in almost all her heroines, save Dinah and Dorothea, who are evoluted from the beginning, paints the gradual evolution of a soul by the ennobling influence of a higher mind and a religious love.

We come now to a curious little crop of errors. Though so profound a scholar—being indeed too learned for perfect artistry—she makes strange mistakes for a master of the language such as she was. She spells "insistence" with an "a," and she gives a superfluous "c" to "Machiavelli."

By MRS. LYNN LINTON

She sometimes permits herself to slip into the literary misdemeanour of no nominative to her sentence, and into the graver sin of making a singular verb govern the plural noun of a series. She says "frightened at" and "under circumstances"; "by the sly" and "down upon"; and she follows "neither" with "or," as also "never" and "not." She is "averse to"; she has even been known to split her infinitive, and to say "and which" without remorse. Once she condescends to the iniquity of "proceeding to take," than which "commencing" is only one stage lower in literary vulgarity; and many of her sentences are as clumsy as a clown's dancing-steps. As no one can accuse her of either ignorance or indifference, still less of haste and slap-dash, these small flaws in the great jewel of her genius are instructive instances of the clinging effect of our carelessness in daily speech; so that grammatical inaccuracy becomes as a second nature to us, and has to be unlearned by all who write.

Nevertheless, with all her faults fully acknowledged and honestly shown, we ever return as to an inexhaustible fountain, to her greatness of thought, her supreme power, her nobility of aim, her matchless humour, her magnificent drawing, her wise philosophy, her accurate learning—as profound as it was accurate. Though we do not bracket her with Plato and Kant, as did one of her

GEORGE ELIOT

panegyrists, nor hold her equal to Fielding for naturalness, nor to Scott for picturesqueness, nor as able as was Thackeray to project herself into the conditions of thought and society of times other than her own, we do hold her as the sceptred queen of our English Victorian authoresses—superior even to Charlotte Brontë, to Mrs. Gaskell, to Harriet Martineau—formidable rivals as these are to all others, living or dead.

If she had not crossed that Rubicon, or, having crossed it, had been content with more complete insurgency than she was, she would have been a happier woman and a yet more finished novelist. As things were, her life and principles were at cross-corners; and when her literary success had roused up her social ambition, and fame had lifted her far above the place where her birth had set her, she realised the mistake she had made. Then the sense of inharmoniousness between what she was and what she would have been did, to some degree, react on her work, to the extent at least of killing in it all passion and spontaneity. Her whole life and being were moulded to an artificial pose, and the "made" woman could not possibly be the spontaneous artist. Her yet more fatal blunder of marrying an obscure individual many years younger than herself, and so destroying the poetry of her first union by destroying its sense of continuity and constancy, would have

By MRS. LYNN LINTON

still more disastrously reacted on her work had she lived. She died in time, for anything below "Theophrastus Such" would have seriously endangered her fame and lessened her greatness—culminating as this did in "Middlemarch," the best and grandest of her novels, from the zenith of which "Daniel Deronda," her last, is a sensible decline.

E. Lynn Linton.

MRS. GASKELL

By EDNA LYALL

MRS. GASKELL

OF all the novelists of Queen Victoria's reign there is not one to whom the present writer turns with such a sense of love and gratitude as to Mrs. Gaskell. This feeling is undoubtedly shared by thousands of men and women, for about all the novels there is that wonderful sense of sympathy, that broad human interest which appeals to readers of every description. The hard-worked little girl in the schoolroom can forget the sorrows of arithmetic or the vexations of French verbs as she pores over "Wives and Daughters" on a Saturday half-holiday, and, as George Sand remarked to Lord Houghton, this same book, "Wives and Daughters," "would rivet the attention of the most *blasé* man of the world."

With the exception of her powerful "Life of Charlotte Brontë," Mrs. Gaskell wrote only novels or short stories.

MRS. GASKELL

The enormous difficulties which attended the writing of a biography of the author of "Jane Eyre" would, we venture to think, have baffled any other writer of that time. It is easy now, years after Charlotte Brontë's death, to criticise the wisdom of this or that page, to hunt up slight mistakes, to maintain that in some details Mrs. Gaskell was wrong. To be wise too late is an easy and, to some apparently, a most grateful task; but it would, nevertheless, be hard to find a biography of more fascinating interest, or one which more successfully grappled with the great difficulty of the undertaking.

As Mr. Clement Shorter remarks, the "Life of Charlotte Brontë" "ranks with Boswell's 'Life of Johnson' and Lockhart's 'Life of Scott.'" It is pleasant, too, to read Charlotte Brontë's own words in a letter to Mr. Williams, where she mentions her first letter from her future friend and biographer:

"The letter you forwarded this morning was from Mrs. Gaskell, authoress of 'Mary Barton.' She said I was not to answer it, but I cannot help doing so. The note brought the tears to my eyes. She is a good, she is a great woman. Proud am I that I can touch a chord of sympathy in souls so noble. In Mrs. Gaskell's nature it mournfully pleases me to fancy a remote affinity to my sister Emily. In Miss Martineau's mind I have always felt the same, though there are wide differences. Both these ladies are above me—certainly far my superiors in attainments and experience. I think I could look up to them if I knew them."

For lovers of the author of "Mary Barton" it is hard, however, not to feel a grudge against the "Life of Charlotte Brontë"—or, rather, the reception accorded to it. Owing to the violent attacks to which it gave rise, to a threatened action for libel on the part of some of those mentioned in the book, and to the manifold annoyances to which the publication of the Biography subjected the writer, Mrs. Gaskell determined that no record of her own life should be written.

It is pleasant to find that there were gleams of light mixed with the many vexations. Charles Kingsley writes to Mrs. Gaskell in warm appreciation of the "Life":

"Be sure," he says, "that the book will do good. It will shame literary people into some stronger belief that a simple, virtuous, practical home-life is consistent with high imaginative genius; and it will shame, too, the prudery of a not over-cleanly, though carefully whitewashed, age, into believing that purity is now (as in all ages till now) quite compatible with the knowledge of evil. I confess that the book has made me ashamed of myself. 'Jane Eyre' I hardly looked into, very seldom reading a work of fiction—yours, indeed, and Thackeray's are the only ones I care to open. 'Shirley' disgusted me at the opening, and I gave up the writer and her books with the notion that she was a person who liked coarseness. How I misjudged her! and how thankful I am that I never put a word of my misconceptions into print, or recorded my misjudgments of one who is a whole heaven above me. Well have you done your work, and given us a picture of a valiant woman made perfect by sufferings. I shall now read carefully and lovingly every word she has written."

Mrs. Gaskell's wish regarding her own biography has, of course, been respected by her family; but the world is the poorer, and it is impossible not to regret that the life of so dearly loved a writer must never be attempted.

The books reveal a mind as delicately pure as a child's, wedded to that true mother's heart which is wide enough to take in all the needy. Looking, moreover, at that goodly row of novels—whether in the dear old shabby volumes that have been read and re-read for years, or in that dainty little set recently published in a case, which the rising generation can enjoy—one cannot help reflecting that here is " A Little Child's Monument," surely the most beautiful memorial of a great love and a great grief that could be imagined. It was not until the death of her little child—the only son of the family—that Mrs. Gaskell, completely broken down by grief, began, at her husband's suggestion, to write. And thus a great sorrow brought forth a rich and wonderful harvest, as grief borne with strength and courage always may do; and the world has good reason to remember that little ten months' child whose short life brought about such great results.

A question naturally suggests itself at this point as to Mrs. Gaskell's birth and education. How far had she inherited her literary gifts? And in what way had her mind been influenced by the surroundings of her childhood and girlhood? Her mother, Mrs. Stevenson, was a Miss Holland, of Sandlebridge, in Cheshire; her father—William Stevenson—was at first classical tutor in the Manchester Academy, and later on, during his residence in Edinburgh, was editor of the *Scots Magazine* and a frequent contributor to the *Edinburgh Review*. He was next appointed Keeper of the Records to the Treasury, an appointment which caused his removal from Edinburgh to Chelsea; and it was there, in Cheyne Row, that Elizabeth Cleghorn Stevenson, the future novelist, was born.

Owing to the death of her mother, she was adopted when only a month old by her aunt, Mrs. Lumb, and taken to Knutsford, in Cheshire, the little town so wonderfully described in "Cranford." For two years in her girlhood she was educated at Stratford-on-Avon, walking in the flowery meadows where Shakspere once walked, worshipping in the stately old church where he worshipped, and where he willed that his body should be left at rest; nor is it possible to help imagining that the associations of that ideal place had an influence on the mind of the future writer, doing something to give that essentially English tone which characterises all her books.

After her father's second marriage she went to live with him, and her education was superintended by him until his death in 1829, when she once more returned to Knutsford. Here, at the age of twenty-two, she was married to the Rev. William Gaskell, M.A., of Cross Street Chapel, Manchester; and Manchester remained her home ever after.

Such are the brief outlines of a life story which was to have such a wide and lasting influence for good. For nothing is more striking than this when we think over the well-known novels—they are not only consummate works of art, full of literary charm, perfect in style and rich with the most delightful humour and pathos—they are books from which that morbid lingering over the loathsome details of vice, those sensuous descriptions of sin too rife in the novels of the present day, are altogether excluded.

Not that the stories are namby-pamby, or unreal in any sense; they are wholly free from the horrid prudery, the Pharisaical temper, which makes a merit of walking through life in blinkers and refuses to know of anything that can shock the respectable. Mrs. Gaskell was too genuine an artist to fall either into this error or into the error of bad taste and want of reserve. She drew life with utter reverence; she held the highest of all ideals, and she dared to be true.

How tender and womanly and noble, for instance, is her treatment of the difficult subject which forms the *motif* of "Ruth"! How sorrowfully true to life is the story of the dressmaker's apprentice with no place in which to spend her Sunday afternoons! We seem ourselves to breathe the dreadful "stuffy" atmosphere of the workroom, to feel the dreary monotony of the long day's work. It is so natural that the girl's fancy should be caught by Henry Bellingham, who was courteous to her when she mended the torn dress of his partner at the ball; so inevitable that she should lose her heart to him when she witnessed his gallant rescue of the drowning child. But her fall was not inevitable, and one of the finest bits in the whole novel is the description of Ruth's hesitation in the inn parlour when, finding herself most cruelly and unjustly cast off by her employer, she has just accepted her lover's suggestion that she shall go with him to London, little guessing what the promise involved, yet intuitively feeling that her consent had been unwise.

"Ruth became as hot as she had previously been cold, and went and opened the window, and leant out into the still, sweet evening air. The bush of sweetbriar underneath the window scented the place, and the delicious fragrance reminded her of her old home. I think scents affect and quicken the memory even more than either sights or sounds; for Ruth had instantly before her eyes the little garden beneath the window of her mother's room, with the old man leaning on his stick watching her, just as he had done not three hours before on that very afternoon." She remembers the faithful love of the old labouring man and his wife who had served her parents in their lifetime, and for their sake would help and advise her now. Would it not be better to go to them?

"She put on her bonnet and opened the parlour door; but then she saw the square figure of the landlord standing at the open house door, smoking his evening pipe, and looming large and distinct against the dark air and landscape beyond. Ruth remembered the cup of tea that she had drunk; it must be paid for, and she had no money with her. She feared that he would not let her leave the house without paying. She thought that she would leave a note for Mr. Bellingham saying where she was gone, and how she had left the house in debt, for (like a child) all dilemmas appeared of equal magnitude to her; and the difficulty of passing the landlord while he stood there, and of giving him an explanation of the circumstances, appeared insuperable, and as awkward and fraught with inconvenience as far more serious situations. She kept peeping out of her room after she had written her little pencil note, to see if the outer door was still obstructed. There he stood motionless, enjoying his pipe, and looking out into the darkness which gathered thick with the coming night. The fumes of the tobacco were carried into the house and brought back Ruth's sick headache. Her energy left her; she became stupid and languid, and incapable of spirited exertion; she modified her plan of action to the determination of asking Mr. Bellingham to take her to Milham Grange, to the care of her humble friends, instead of to London. And she thought in her simplicity that he would instantly consent when he had heard her reasons."

The selfishness of the man who took advantage of her weakness and ignorance is finely drawn because it is not at all exaggerated. Henry Bellingham is no monster of wickedness, but a man with many fine qualities spoilt by an over-indulgent and unprincipled mother, and yielding too easily to her worldly-wise arguments.

Ruth first sees a faint trace of his selfishness—she calls it "unfairness"—when, on their arrival in Wales, he persuades the landlady to give them rooms in the hotel and to turn out on a false pretext some other guests into the *dépendance* across the road. She understands his selfish littleness of soul only too well when, years after, she talks to him during that wonderfully described interview in the chapter called "The Meeting on the Sands." He cannot in the least understand her. "The deep sense of penitence she expressed he took for earthly shame, which he imagined he could soon soothe away." He actually has the audacity to tempt her a second time; then, after her indignant refusal, he offers her marriage. To his great amazement she refuses this too. "Why, what on earth makes you say that?" asked he . . . .

"I do not love you. I did once. Don't say I did not love you then; but I do not now. I could never love you again. All you have said and done since you came to Abermouth has only made me wonder how I ever could have loved you. We are very far apart; the time that has pressed down my life like brands of hot iron, and scarred me for ever, has been nothing to you. You have talked of it with no sound of moaning in your voice, no shadow over the brightness of your face; it has left no sense of sin on your conscience, while me it haunts and haunts; and yet I might plead that I was an ignorant child; only I will not plead anything, for God knows all. But this is only one piece of our great difference."

"You mean that I am no saint," he said, impatient at her speech. "Granted. But people who are no saints have made very good husbands before now. Come, don't let any morbid, overstrained conscientiousness interfere with substantial happiness—happiness both to you and to me—for I am sure I can make you happy—ay! and make you love me too, in spite of your pretty defiance. . . . . And here are advantages for Leonard, to be gained by you quite in a holy and legitimate way."

She stood very erect.

"If there was one thing needed to confirm me, you have named it. You shall have nothing to do with my boy by my consent, much less by my agency. I would rather see him working on the roadside than leading such a life—being such a one as you are. . . . . If at last I have spoken out too harshly and too much in a spirit of judgment, the fault is yours. If there were no other reason to prevent our marriage but the one fact that it would bring Leonard into contact with you, that would be enough."

Later on, a fever visits the town, and Ruth becomes a nurse. When she hears that the father of her child is ill and untended she volunteers to nurse him, and, being already worn out with work, she dies in consequence. The man's smallness of mind, his contemptible selfishness, are finely indicated in the scene where he goes to look at Ruth as she lies dead.

He was "disturbed" by the distress of the old servant Sally, and saying, "Come, my good woman! we must all die," *tries to console her with a sovereign!!*

The old servant turns upon him indignantly, then "bent down and kissed the lips from whose marble, unyielding touch he recoiled even in thought." At that moment the old minister, who had sheltered Ruth in her trouble, enters. Henry makes many offers to him as to providing for Ruth's child, Leonard, and says, "I cannot tell you how I regret that she should have died in consequence of her love to me." But from gentle old Mr. Benson he receives only an icy refusal, and the stern words, "Men may call such actions as yours youthful follies. There is another name for them with God."

The sadness of the book is relieved by the delightful humour of Sally, the servant. The account of the wooing of Jeremiah Dixon is a masterpiece; and Sally's hesitation when, having found her proof against the attractions of "a four-roomed house, furniture conformable, and eighty pounds a year," her lover mentions the pig that will be ready for killing by Christmas, is a delicious bit of comedy.

"Well, now! would you believe it? the pig were a temptation. I'd a receipt for curing hams. . . . However, I resisted. Says I, very stern, because I felt I'd been wavering, 'Master Dixon, once for all, pig or no pig, I'll not marry you.'"

The description of the minister's home is very beautiful. Here are a few lines which show in what its charm consisted:

"In the Bensons' house there was the same unconsciousness of individual merit, the same absence of introspection and analysis of motive, as there had been in her mother; but it seemed that their lives were pure and good not merely from a lovely and beautiful nature, but from some law the obedience to which was of itself harmonious peace, and which governed them. . . . This household had many failings; they were but human, and, with all their loving desire to bring their lives into harmony with the will of God, they often erred and fell short. But somehow the very errors and faults of one individual served to call out higher excellences in another; and so they reacted upon each other, and the result of short discords was exceeding harmony and peace."

MRS. GASKELL

The publication of "Ruth," with its brave, outspoken words, its fearless demand for one standard of morality for men and women, subjected the author to many attacks, as we may gather from the following warm-hearted letter by Charles Kingsley :

"*July* 25, 1853.

"I am sure that you will excuse my writing to you thus abruptly when you read the cause of my writing. I am told, to my great astonishment, that you had heard painful speeches on account of 'Ruth'; what was told me raised all my indignation and disgust. . . . Among all my large acquaintance I never heard, or have heard, but one unanimous opinion of the beauty and righteousness of the book, and that above all from really good women. If you could have heard the things which I heard spoken of it this evening by a thorough High Church, fine lady of the world, and by her daughter, too, as pure and pious a soul as one need see, you would have no more doubt than I have, that, whatsoever the 'snobs' and the bigots may think, English people, in general, have but one opinion of 'Ruth,' and that is, one of utter satisfaction. I doubt not you have had this said to you already often. Believe me, you may have it said to you as often as you will by the purest and most refined of English women. May God bless you, and help you to write many more such books as you have already written, is the fervent wish of your very faithful servant,

"C. KINGSLEY."

"Mary Barton," which was the first of the novels, was published in 1848, and this powerful and fascinating story at once set Mrs. Gaskell in the first rank of English novelists. People differed as to the views set forth in the book, but all were agreed as to its literary force and its great merits. Like "Alton Locke," it has done much to break down class barriers and make the rich try to understand the poor; and when we see the great advance in this direction which has been made since the date of its publication, we are able partly to realise how startling the first appearance of such a book must have been. The secret of the extraordinary power which the book exercises on its readers is, probably, that the writer takes one into the very heart of the life she is describing.

Most books of the sort fail to arrest our attention. Why? Because they are written either as mere "goody" books for parish libraries, and are carefully watered down lest they should prove too sensational and enthralling; or because they are written by people who have only a surface knowledge of the characters they describe and the life they would fain depict. "David Copperfield" is probably the most popular book Dickens ever wrote, and is likely to outlive his other works, just because he himself knew so thoroughly well all that his hero had to pass through, and could draw from real knowledge the characters in the background. And at the present time we are all able to understand the Indian Mutiny in a way that has never been possible before, because Mrs. Steel in her wonderful novel, "On the Face of the Waters," has, through her knowledge of native life, given us a real insight into the heart of a great nation.

Brilliant trash may succeed for two or three seasons, but unless there is in it some germ of real truth which appeals to the heart and conscience it will not live. Sensationalism alone will not hold its ground. There must be in the writer a real deep inner knowledge of his subject if the book is to do its true work. And we venture to think that "Mary Barton," which for nearly half a century has been influencing people all over the world, owes its vitality very largely to the fact that Mrs. Gaskell knew the working people of Manchester, not as a professional doler out of tracts or charitable relief, not in any detestable, patronising way, but knew them as *friends*.

By EDNA LYALL

This surely is the reason why the characters in the novel are so intensely real. What could be finer than the portrait of Mary herself, from the time when we are first introduced to her as the young apprentice to a milliner and dressmaker, to the end of the book, when she has passed through her great agony? How entirely the reader learns to live with her in her brave struggle to prove her lover's innocence! One of the most powerful parts of the book is the description of her plucky pursuit of the good ship *John Cropper*, on board of which was the only man who could save her lover's life by proving an alibi.

But it is not only the leading characters that are so genuine and so true to life. Old Ben Sturgis, the boatman, rough of speech but with more heart than many a smooth-tongued talker; his wife, who sheltered Mary when she had no notion what manner of woman she was; Job Legh, who proved such a good friend to both hero and heroine in their trouble, and whose well-meaning deception of old Mrs. Wilson is so humorously described; John Barton, the father, with the mournful failure at the close of his upright life; old Mr. Carson, the rich father of the murdered man, with his thirst for vengeance, and his tardy but real forgiveness, when he let himself be led by a little child—all these are living men and women, not puppets; while in the character and the tragic story of poor Esther we see the fruits of the writer's deep knowledge of the life of those she helped when released from gaol.

But Mrs. Gaskell looked on both sides of the question. In "North and South," published in 1855, she deals with the labour question from the master's standpoint, and in Mr. Thornton draws a most striking picture of a manufacturer who is just and well-meaning—one who really respects and cares for the men he employs. The main interest of this book lies, however, in the character of the heroine, Margaret, who is placed in a most cruel dilemma by a ne'er-do-well brother whom she shields. By far the most dramatic scene is that in which, to enable Frederick to escape, Margaret tells a deliberate falsehood to the detective who is in search of him. The torture of mind she suffers afterwards for having uttered this intentional lie, and the difficult question whether under any circumstances a lie is warrantable, are dealt with in the writer's most powerful way.

In 1853—the same year in which "Ruth" was published—the greatest of all Mrs. Gaskell's works appeared, the inimitable "Cranford." For humour and for pathos we have nothing like this in all the Victorian literature. It is a book of which one can never tire: yet it can scarcely

By EDNA LYALL

be said to have a plot at all, being just the most delicate miniature painting of a small old-fashioned country town and its inhabitants. What English man or woman is there, however, who will not read and re-read its pages with laughter and tears?

Cranford is said to be in many respects the Knutsford of Mrs. Gaskell's childhood and youth, and there is something so wonderfully lifelike in the descriptions of the manners and customs of the very select little community that one is inclined to believe that there is truth in the assertion. They were gently bred, those old Cranford folk, with their "elegant economy," their hatred of all display, and their considerate tact. There is pathos as well as fun in the description of Mrs. Forrester pretending not to know what cakes were sent up "at a party in her baby-house of a dwelling . . . . though she knew, and we knew, and she knew that we knew, and we knew that she knew that we knew, she had been busy all the morning making tea-bread and sponge-cakes!"

There is an air of leisure and peacefulness in every page of the book, for there was no hurrying life among those dignified old people. "I had often occasion to notice the use that was made of fragments and small opportunities in Cranford: the rose-leaves that were gathered ere they fell to make into a pot-pourri for some one who had no garden; the little bundles of lavender-flowers sent to some town-dweller. Things that many would despise, and actions which it seemed scarcely worth while to perform, were all attended to in Cranford."

Who has not laughed over Miss Betsy Barker's Alderney cow "meekly going to her pasture, clad in dark grey flannel" after her disaster in the lime-pit! or over the masterly description of Miss Jenkyns, who "wore a cravat, and a little bonnet like a jockey-cap, and altogether had the appearance of a strong-minded woman; although she would have despised the modern idea of women being equal to men. Equal, indeed! she knew they were superior."

Dear old Miss Matty, however, with her reverence for the stronger sister, and her love affair of long ago, has a closer hold on the heart of the reader. The description of the meeting of the former lovers is idyllic; and when Thomas Holbrook dies unexpectedly, soon after, the woman whose love-story had been spoilt by the home authorities reverses her own ordinance against "followers" in the case of Martha, the maid-servant, but otherwise makes no sign.

"Miss Matty made a strong effort to conceal her feelings—a concealment she practised even with me, for she has never alluded to Mr. Holbrook again, though the book he gave her lies with her Bible on the little table by her bedside. She did not think I heard her when she asked the little milliner of Cranford to make her caps something like the Honourable Mrs. Jamieson's, or that I noticed the reply:

"'But she wears widows' caps, ma'am!'

"'Oh? I only meant something in that style; not widows', of course, but rather like Mrs. Jamieson's.'"

In the whole book there is not a character that we cannot vividly realise: the Honourable (but sleepy) Mrs. Jamieson; brisk, cheerful Lady Glenmire, who married the sensible country doctor and sacrificed her title to become plain Mrs. Hoggins; Miss Pole, who always with withering scorn called ghosts "indigestion," until the night they heard of the headless lady who had been seen wringing her hands in Darkness Lane, when, to avoid "the woebegone trunk," she with tremulous dignity offered the sedan chairman an extra shilling to go round another way! Captain Brown with his devotion to the writings of Mr. Boz and his feud with Miss Jenkyns as to the superior merits of Dr. Johnson; and Peter, the long-lost brother, who from first to last remains an inveterate practical joker. One and all they become our life-long friends, while the book stands alone as a perfect picture of English country town society fifty years ago.

MRS. GASKELL

Mrs. Gaskell's shorter stories are scarcely equal to the novels, yet some of them are very beautiful. "Cousin Phillis," for example, gives one more of the real atmosphere of country life than any other writer except Wordsworth. We seem actually to smell the new-mown hay as we read the story.

Charming, too, is "My Lady Ludlow" with her genteel horror of dissenters subdued in the end by her genuine good feeling. How often one has longed for that comfortable square pew of hers in the parish church, in which, if she did not like the sermon, she would pull up a glass window as though she had been in her coach, and shut out the sound of the obnoxious preacher! But, with all her peculiarities, she was the most courteous of women—a lady in the true sense of the word—and when people smiled at a shy and untaught visitor who spread out her handkerchief on the front of her dress as the footman handed her coffee, my Lady Ludlow with infinite tact and grace promptly spread *her* handkerchief exactly in the same fashion which the tradesman's wife had adopted.

Among the short tragic stories, the most striking is one called "The Crooked Branch," in which the scene at the assizes has almost unrivalled power; while among the lighter short stories, "My French Master," with its delicate portraiture of the old refugee, and "Mr. Harrison's Confessions," the delightfully written love-story of a young country doctor, are perhaps the most enjoyable.

In 1863 the novel "Sylvia's Lovers" was published, and although, by its fine description of old Whitby and the pathos of the story, it has won many admirers, we infinitely prefer its successor, "Wives and Daughters." There is something very sad in the thought that this last and best of the writer's stories was left unfinished; but happily very little remained to be told, and that little was tenderly touched in to the almost perfect picture of English home life by the daughter who had been not only Mrs. Gaskell's child but her friend. "Wives and Daughters" will always remain as a true and vivid and powerful study of life and character; while Molly Gibson, with her loyal heart and sweet sunshiny nature, will, we venture to think, better represent the majority of English girls than the happily abnormal Dodos and Millicent Chynes of present-day fashion.

In Mr. Gibson's second wife the author has given us a most subtle study of a thoroughly selfish and false-hearted woman, and she is made all the more repulsive because of her outward charms, her soft seductive voice and her lavish employment of terms of endearment. Wonderfully clever, too, is the study of poor little Cynthia, her daughter, whose relations to Molly are most charmingly drawn.

MRS. GASKELL

The story was just approaching its happy and wholesome ending, and the difficulties which had parted Roger Hamley and Molly had just disappeared, when death summoned the writer from a world she had done so much to brighten and to raise. On Sunday evening, November 12, 1865, Mrs. Gaskell died quite suddenly at Holybourne, Alton, Hampshire, a house which she had recently bought as a surprise for her husband. Sad as such a death must always be for those who are left behind, one can imagine nothing happier than " death in harness " for a worker who loves his work.

> " . . . . There's rest above.
> Below let work be death, if work be love ! "

Her " last days," wrote one of those who knew her best, " had been full of loving thought and tender help for others. She was so sweet and dear and noble beyond words." That is the summing-up of the whole ; and, after all, what better could a long biography give us ? The motto of all of us should surely be the words of Mme. Viardot Garcia : " First I am a woman . . . . then I am an artist." And assuredly Mrs. Gaskell's life was ruled on those lines.

" It was wonderful "—wrote her daughter, Mrs. Holland, in a letter to me the other day—" how her writing never interfered with her social or domestic duties. I think she was the best and most practical housekeeper I ever came across, and the brightest, most agreeable hostess, to say nothing of being everything as a mother and friend. She combined both, being my mother and greatest friend in a way you do not often, I think, find between mother and daughter."

Some people are fond of rashly asserting that the ideal wife and mother cares little and knows less about the world beyond the little world of home. Mrs. Gaskell, however, took a keen interest in the questions of the day, and was a Liberal in politics ; while it is quite evident that neither these wider interests nor her philanthropic work tended to interfere with the home life, which was clearly of the noblest type.

The friend as well as the mother of her children, the sharer of all her husband's interests, she yet found time to use to the utmost the great literary gift that had been entrusted to her ; while her sympathy for those in trouble was shown not only in the powerful pleading of her novels, but in quiet, practical work in connection with prisoners. She was one of the fellow labourers of Thomas Wright, the well-known prison philanthropist, and was able to help in finding places for young girls who had been discharged from prison. For working women she also held classes, and both among the poor and the rich had many close friendships.

How far the characters in the novels were studied from life is a question which naturally suggests itself; and Mrs. Holland replies to it as follows: " I do not think my mother ever *consciously* took her characters from special individuals, but we who knew often thought we recognised people, and would tell her, ' Oh, so and so is just like Mr. Blank,' or something of that kind ; and she would say, ' So it is, but I never meant it for him.' And really many of the characters are from originals, or rather are like originals, but they were not consciously meant to be like."

For another detail which will interest Mrs. Gaskell's fellow workers I am indebted to the same source:

"Sometimes she planned her novels more or less beforehand, but in many cases, certainly in that of 'Wives and Daughters,' she had very little plot made beforehand, but planned her story as she wrote. She generally wrote in the morning, but sometimes late at night, when the house was quiet."

Few writers, we think, have exercised a more thoroughly wholesome influence over their readers than Mrs. Gaskell. Her books, with their wide human sympathies, their tender comprehension of human frailty, their bright flashes of humour and their infinite pathos, seem to plead with us to

By EDNA LYALL

love one another. Through them all we seem to hear the author's voice imploring us to "seize the day" and to "make friends," as she does in actual words at the close of one of her Christmas stories, adding pathetically: "I ask it of you for the sake of that old angelic song, heard so many years ago by the shepherds, keeping watch by night on Bethlehem Heights."

A. E. Bayly.
'Edna Lyall.'

MRS. CROWE. MRS. ARCHER CLIVE. MRS. HENRY WOOD

By ADELINE SERGEANT

MRS. CROWE. MRS. ARCHER CLIVE. MRS. HENRY WOOD

MRS. CATHERINE CROWE, whose maiden name was Stevens, was born at Borough Green, in Kent, about 1800, and died in 1876. She married Colonel Crowe in 1822, and took up her residence with him in Edinburgh. Her books were written chiefly between the years 1838 and 1859, and she is best known by her novel, "Susan Hopley," and her collection of ghost stories, "The Night Side of Nature." She was a woman of considerable ability, which appears, however, to have run into rather obscure and sombre channels, such as showed a somewhat morbid bent of mind, with a tendency towards depression, which culminated at last in a short but violent attack of insanity. But love of the unseen and supernatural does not seem to have blunted her keenness of observation in ordinary life, for her novels, the scenes of which are laid chiefly among homely and domestic surroundings, display alike soundness of judgment and considerable dramatic power. As a writer, indeed, Mrs. Crowe was extremely versatile; she wrote plays, children's stories, short historical tales, romantic novels, as well as the ghost stories with which her name seems chiefly to be associated in the minds of this generation. It is evident too, that she believed herself—rightly or wrongly—to be possessed of great philosophical discrimination; but it must be acknowledged that her philosophical and metaphysical studies often led her into curious byways of speculation, into which the reader does not willingly wander.

It is worth noting that Mrs. Crowe's ideas respecting the status and education of women were, for the days in which she lived, exceedingly "advanced." In "Lilly Dawson," for instance, a story published in 1847, she makes an elaborate protest against the kind of education which women were then receiving. "It is true," she says, "that there is little real culture amongst men; there are few strong minds and fewer honest ones, but they have still more advantages. If their education has been bad, it has at least been a trifle better than ours. Six hours a day at Latin and Greek are better than six hours

By ADELINE SERGEANT

a day at worsted work and embroidery ; and time is better spent in acquiring a smattering of mathematics than in strumming Hook's lessons on a bad pianoforte."

Her views of women in general are well expressed in the following words from the same work of fiction. " If, as we believe, under no system of training, the intellect of woman would be found as strong as that of a man, she is compensated by her intuitions being stronger. If her reason be less majestic, her insight is clearer ; where man reasons she sees. Nature, in short, gave her all that was needful to enable her to play a noble part in the world's history, if man would but let her play it out, and not treat her like a full-grown baby, to be flattered and spoilt on the one hand, and coerced and restricted on the other, vibrating between royal rule and slavish serfdom." Surely we hear the voice of Nora Helmer herself, the very quintessence of Ibsenism! It must have required considerable courage to write in this way in the year 1847, and Mrs. Crowe should certainly be numbered among the lovers of educational reform. In many ways she seems to have been a woman of strong individuality and decided opinions.

Her first work was a drama, " Aristodemus," published anonymously in 1838 ; it showed considerable ability and was well regarded by the critics. She then wrote a novel, "Men and Women, or Manorial Rights," in 1839; and in 1841 published her most successful work of fiction: "Susan Hopley, or the Adventures of a Maid-servant." This story was more generally popular than any other from her pen, but it is to be doubted whether it possesses more literary ability or points of greater interest than the rest.

Mrs. Crowe then embarked upon a translation of "The Seeress of Provorst," by Justinus Kerner, a book of revelations concerning the inner life of man; and in 1848 she published a book called "The Night Side of Nature," a collection of supernatural tales gathered from many sources, probably the best storehouse of ghost stories in the English language. Its interest is a little marred by the credulity of the author. She seems never to disbelieve any ghost story of any kind that comes in her way. From the humble apologies, however, with which she opens her dissertation on the subject, it is easy to see how great a change has passed over people's minds in the course of the last fifty years, with respect to the supernatural. If Mrs. Crowe had lived in these days, she would have found herself in intimate relations with the Society for Psychical Research, and would have had no reason to excuse herself for the choice of her subject.

By ADELINE SERGEANT

She divides her book into sections, which treat of dreams (where we get Sir Noel Paton's account of his mother's curious vision); warnings; double-dreaming and trance, with the stories of Colonel Townshend's voluntary trance and the well-known legend of Lord Balcarres and the ghost of Claverhouse; doppel-gängers and apparitions (including the stories of Lady Beresford's branded wrist and Lord Lyttleton's warning); and other chapters descriptive of haunted houses, with details concerning clairvoyance and the use of the crystal. It is interesting to find among these the original account of "Pearlin Jean," of which Miss Sarah Tytler has made such excellent use in one of her recent books. An account of the phenomena of *stigmata*, and the case of Catherine Emmerich, are also described in detail. Lovers of the supernatural will find much to gratify their taste in a perusal of "The Night Side of Nature."

Mrs. Crowe did not exhaust the subject in this volume, for she issued a book on ghosts and family legends, a volume for Christmas, in the year 1859; a work full of the kind of stories which became so popular in the now almost obsolete Christmas Annual of succeeding years. It is also curious to note, that in 1848, Mrs. Crowe produced a work of an entirely different nature, namely, an excellent story for children, entitled "Pippie's

Warning, or Mind Your Temper"—another instance of her versatility of mind.

"The Adventures of a Beauty" and "Light and Darkness" appeared in 1852. The latter is a collection of short tales from different sources, partly historical and partly imaginative, and certainly more in accordance with the taste of modern days than her elaborate domestic stories. Mrs. Crowe's taste for the horrible is distinctly perceptible in this collection. There is an account of the celebrated poisoners, Frau Gottfried, Madame Ursinus, and Margaret Zwanziger, whose crimes were so numerous that they themselves forgot the number of their victims; and of Mr. Tinius, who went about making morning calls and murdering the persons whom he honoured with a visit. The histories of Lesurques, the hero of the "Lyons Mail," and of Madame Louise, Princess of France, who became a nun, are well narrated; but nearly all the stories are concerned with horrors such as suggest the productions of Mr. Wilkie Collins. "The Priest of St. Quentin" and "The Lycanthropist" are two of the most powerful.

Her next novel, a more purely domestic one, was "Linny Lockwood," issued in 1854. A sentence from the preface to this book anticipates—rather early, as we may think—the approaching death of the three-volume novel:

By ADELINE SERGEANT

"Messrs. Routledge and Co. have been for some time soliciting me to write them an original novel for their cheap series; and being convinced that the period for publishing at £1 11s. 6d., books of a kind that people generally read but once, is gone by, I have resolved to make the experiment."

She wrote another tragedy, "The Cruel Kindness," in 1853, and abridged "Uncle Tom's Cabin" for children. In 1859 a pamphlet on "Spiritualism and the Age we Live in," constituted the last of her more important works, although she continued, for some time after recovery from the attack of insanity which we have mentioned, to write papers and stories for periodicals.

In spite of Mrs. Crowe's love for the supernatural and the horrible, she is one of the pioneers of the purely domestic story—that story of the affections and the emotions peculiar to the Victorian Age. She is allied to the schools of Richardson and Fanny Burney rather than to those of Sir Walter Scott or Miss Austen; for although her incidents are often romantic and even far-fetched, her characters are curiously homely and generally of humble environment. Thus, for instance, "Susan Hopley" is a maid-servant (though not of the Pamela kind nor with the faintest resemblance to Esther Waters); Lilly Dawson, although proved ultimately to be the daughter of a colonel, passes the greater part of her earlier life as a drudge and a dependent; and Linny Lockwood, while refined and educated, is reduced to the situation of a lady's maid. The circumstances of her heroines are, as a rule, extremely prosaic, and would possibly have been condemned by writers of Miss Austen's school as hopelessly vulgar; but Mrs. Crowe's way of treating these characters and their surroundings bears upon it no stamp of vulgarity at all. Its great defect is its want of humour to light up the sordid side of the life which she describes. She is almost always serious, full of exalted and occasionally overstrained sentiment. And even when treating of childhood, it is rarely that she relaxes so far as (in "Lilly Dawson") to describe the naughtiness of the little girl who insisted upon praying for the cat. This is almost the sole glimpse of a sense of fun to which Mrs. Crowe treats us in her numerous volumes.

To the present age "Susan Hopley," although so popular at the time of its publication, is less attractive than the stories of "Linny Lockwood" and "Lilly Dawson." The form adopted for the recital of Susan's narrative is extremely inartistic, for it comprises Susan's reminiscences, interspersed at intervals with narrative, and supposed to be told by her in mature age, when she is housekeeper to the hero of the story. Nevertheless, the plot is ingenious, turning on the murder of Susan's brother by a handsome and gentlemanly villain, and the subsequent exposure of his guilt by means of Susan's energy and the repentance of one of his victims. It has all the elements of a sensational story, with the exception of a "sympathetic" heroine or any other really interesting character; for Susan Hopley, the embodiment of all homely virtues, is distinctly dull, and it is difficult to feel the attractiveness of the "beautiful and haughty" dairymaid, Mabel Lightfoot, whose frailty forms an important element in the discovery of Gaveston's guilt.

"Lilly Dawson" may be said to possess something of a psychological interest, which redeems it from the charge of dulness brought against "Susan Hopley." The heroine is thrown as a child into the hands of a wild and lawless family, smugglers and desperadoes, who make of her a household slave; and the child appears at first to be utterly stupid and apathetic. A touch of affection and sympathy is needed before her intellect awakes. In fear of being forced to marry one of the sons of the house in which she has been brought up, when she is only fifteen, she escapes from her enemies, becomes the guide and adopted child of an old blind man, takes service as a nursemaid, is employed in a milliner's workroom, narrowly escapes being murdered by the man whom she refused to marry, and finally acts as maid in the house of her own relations, where she is discovered and received with the greatest affection. Nevertheless, she cannot endure the life of "a fine lady," and goes back ultimately to marry the humble lover whose kindness had cheered her in the days of her childhood and poverty.

In "Linny Lockwood" there is a touch of emotion, even of passion, which is wanting in the previous stories. It embraces scenes and situations which are quite as moving as any which thrilled the English public in the pages of "Jane Eyre" or "East Lynne," but, owing possibly to Mrs. Crowe's obstinate realism and somewhat didactic homeliness of diction and sentiment, it seems somewhat to have missed its mark. Linny Lockwood marries a man entirely unworthy of her, whose love strays speedily from her to another woman—a married woman with whom he elopes and whom he afterwards abandons. Linny, being poor and destitute, looks about for work, and takes the post of maid to her husband's deserted mistress, without, of course, knowing what had been the connection between them. But before the birth of Kate's child, Linny learns the truth and nevertheless remains with her to soothe her weakness, and lessen the pangs of remorse of which the poor woman ultimately dies. A full explanation between the two women takes place before Kate's death; and the child that is left behind is adopted by Linny Lockwood, who refuses to pardon the husband, who sues to her for forgiveness, or to live with him again.

The character of Linny Lockwood is a very beautiful one, and the story appeals to the reader's sensibilities more strongly than the recital of Susan Hopley's adventures or the girlish sorrows of Lilly Dawson.

Mrs. Crowe's writings certainly heralded the advent of a new kind of fiction: a kind which has been, perhaps more than any other, characteristic of the early years of the Victorian Age. It is the literature of domestic realism, of homely unromantic characters, which no accessories of exciting adventure can render interesting or remarkable in themselves—characters distinguished by every sort of virtue, yet not possessed of any ideal attractiveness. She is old-fashioned enough to insist upon a happy ending, to punish the wicked and to reward the good. But amid all the conventionality of her style, one is conscious of a note of hard common sense and a power of seeing things as they really are, which in these days would probably have forced her (perhaps against her will) into the realistic school. She seems, in fact, to hover between two ages of literature, and to be possessed at times of two different spirits—one the romantic and the supernatural, the other distinctly commonplace and workaday. Perhaps it is by the former that she will be chiefly remembered, but it is through the latter that she takes a place in English literature. She left a mark upon the age in which she lived, and she helped, in a quiet, undemonstrative fashion, to mould the women of England after higher ideals than had been possible in the early days of the century. Those who consider the development of women to be one of the distinguishing features of Queen Victoria's reign should not forget that they owe deep gratitude to writers like Mrs. Crowe, who upheld the standard of a woman's right to education and economic independence long before these subjects were discussed in newspapers and upon public platforms. For, as George Eliot has said, with her usual wisdom, it is owing to the labours of those who have lived in comparative obscurity and lie in forgotten graves, that things are well with us here and now.

By ADELINE SERGEANT

CAROLINE CLIVE was the second daughter and co-heiress of Edmund Meysey-Wigley, of Shakenhurst, Worcestershire. She was born in 1801, at Brompton Green, London, and was married in 1840 to the Rev. Archer Clive, Rector of Solihull, Warwickshire. In the latest edition of her poems, her daughter states that " Mrs. Archer Clive, from a severe illness when she was three years old, was lame ; and though her strong mind and high spirit carried her happily through childhood and early life, as she grew up she felt sharply the loss of all the active pleasures enjoyed by others."

Her novel, " Paul Ferroll," contains a touching poem which shows how deeply she felt the privations consequent on her infirmity.

" Gaeta's orange groves were there
    Half circling round the sun-kissed sea ;
And all were gone and left the fair
    Rich garden solitude but me.

" My feeble feet refused to tread
    The rugged pathway to the bay ;
Down the steep rocky way they tread
    And gain the boat and glide away.

*   *   *   *   *

MRS. ARCHER CLIVE

" Above me hung the golden glow
 Of fruit which is at one with flowers;
Below me gleamed the ocean's flow,
 Like sapphires in the midday hours.

" A passing by there was of wings,
 Of silent, flower-like butterflies;
The sudden beetle as it springs
 Full of the life of southern skies.

  * * * * *

" It was an hour of bliss to die,
 But not to sleep, for ever came
The warm thin air, and, passing by,
 Fanned sense and soul and heart to flame."

A great love of nature and a yearning to tread its scenes breathe in every word of these lines, which possess an essentially pathetic charm of their own.

Mrs. Clive died in July 1873, from the result of an accident, by which her dress was set on fire when she was writing in her boudoir at Whitfield, with her books and papers around her. Her health was extremely delicate, and she had been for many years a confirmed invalid.

Her first work consisted of the well-known " IX Poems by V." published in 1840. These poems were very favourably received, and were much praised by Dugald Stewart, by Lockhart, and by Mr. Gladstone, who says of them, " They form a small book, which is the life and soul of a great book." They were also very favourably reviewed in the *Quarterly* (LXVI. 408-11). Her other poems, "I Watch the Heavens," "The Queen's Ball," "The Vale of the Rea," etc., have been re-published with the original "IX" in a separate volume. "Year After Year," published in 1858, passed into two editions; but Mrs. Clive's reputation chiefly rests upon her story of "Paul Ferroll," published in 1855, and its sequel, "Why Paul Ferroll Killed his Wife." The second story was, however, in no way equal to the first; and a subsequent novel, "John Greswold," which appeared in 1864, was decidedly inferior to its predecessors, although containing passages of considerable literary merit.

"Paul Ferroll" has passed through several editions, and has been translated into French. It was not until the fourth edition that the concluding chapter, which brings the story down to the death of Paul Ferroll, was added.

There is little difference in date between the writings of Mrs. Crowe and those of Mrs. Archer Clive, but there is a tremendous gap between their methods and the tone of their novels. As a matter of fact they belong to different generations, in spite of their similarity of age. Mrs. Crowe belongs to the older school of fictionists, while Mrs. Archer Clive is curiously modern. The tone and style are like the tone and style of the present day, not so much in the dialogue, which is generally stilted, after the fashion of the age in which she lived, as in the mental attitude of the characters, in the atmosphere of the books, and the elaborate, sometimes even artistic, collocation of scenes and incidents.

"Paul Ferroll" is often looked upon merely as a novel of plot, almost the first "sensational" novel, as we call it, of the century. But it is more than that. There is a distinct working out of character and a subordination of mere incident to its development; and the original ending was of so striking and pathetic a nature that we can only regret the subsequent addition, which probably the influence of others made necessary, just as in "Villette" Charlotte Brontë was obliged to soften down her own conception, in order to satisfy the conventional requirements of her friends.

The story of "Paul Ferroll" displays a good deal of constructive skill, although the mystery enfolded in its pages is more easily penetrated than would be the case in a modern sensational novel. The fact is, we have increased our knowledge of the intricacies both of human nature and of criminal law in these latter days, and our novelists are cleverer in concealing or half revealing their mysteries than they were in "the forties." For a few pages, at least, the reader may be deluded into the belief that Paul Ferroll is a worthy and innocent man, and that his wife has been murdered by some revengeful servant or ruffianly vagabond. But the secret of his guilt is too speedily fathomed; and from that point to the end of the book, the question turns on the possibilities of its discovery or the likelihood and effects of his own confession.

Mrs. Clive's picture of the "bold bad man" is not so successful as that of Charlotte Brontë's Rochester. Rochester, with all his faults, commands sympathy, but our sympathies are alienated from Paul Ferroll when we find (in the first chapter) that he could ride out tranquilly on a summer's morning, scold his gardener, joke with the farmer's wife, and straighten out the farmer's accounts, when he had just previously murdered his wife in her sleep by thrusting a sharp pointed knife through her head "below the ear." Even although he afterwards exhibits agitation on being brought face to face with the corpse of his wife, we cannot rid ourselves of our remembrance of the insensibility which he had shown. The motive for the crime is not far to seek. He had fixed his affections on a young girl, his marriage with whom had been prevented by the woman who became his wife.

MRS. ARCHER CLIVE

Dissension and increasing bitterness grew up between the pair; and her death was held as a release by Paul Ferroll, who hastened to bring home, as his second wife, the girl whom he had formerly loved.

No suspicion attached to him, and he is careful to provide means of defence for the labourer Franks and his wife, who have been accused of the murder. On returning home with his second wife, to whom he is passionately attached, he devotes himself entirely to literary pursuits, refusing to mix with any of the society of the place. From time to time his motive is allowed to appear; he has determined never to accept a favour from, nor become a friend of, the country gentlemen, with whom he is thrown into contact, so that they shall never have to say, supposing the truth should ever be acknowledged, that he has made his way into their houses on false pretences. But in spite of his seclusion, he lives a life of ideal happiness with his wife, Ellinor, and their beautiful little child, Janet, who, however, occupies quite a secondary place in the hearts of her father and mother, who are wrapt up in one another.

The events of the next few years are not treated in detail, although there is at one point a most interesting description of the state of a town in which cholera rages, when Paul Ferroll flings himself with heroic ardour into every effort to stem the tide of the disease. Owing to a riot at the time of the Assizes, Ferroll fires on one of the crowd and kills him, so that by a curious coincidence, he is tried for murder, and has full experience of the horrors accompanying the situation of a criminal. He is sentenced to death but pardoned, and returns to his old life at home. The widow of the labourer who had formerly been accused of the murder of his first wife then returns to England, and Ferroll knows that her return increases the danger of discovery. He tries to escape it by going abroad, but finds on his return that Martha Franks, the widow, is in possession of some trinkets which belonged to the late Mrs. Ferroll, that she has been accused of theft and finally of the murder of her mistress. This is the very conjuncture which had always appeared possible to Paul Ferroll; the moment has come when he feels himself obliged to confess the truth, in order to save a fellow creature from unjust condemnation. He thereupon acknowledges his guilt, is at once conveyed to prison, and after a merely formal trial is condemned to death—the execution to take place, apparently, in three days, according to the inhuman custom of the time.

Ellinor dies on the day when she hears of his confession; and Janet, his daughter, now eighteen years old, and Janet's young lover, Hugh Bartlett, are the only persons who remain faithful to him or make efforts for his safety. Through Hugh's efforts and the treachery of the gaoler, Paul Ferroll manages, in a somewhat improbable manner, to escape from prison; and he and Janet make their way to Spain, whence they will be able to take ship for America.

The conclusion of the story, as at first written, is particularly striking. Janet, after an illness, has come to herself: "She did not know the place where she was. The air was warm and perfumed, the windows shaded, the room quite a stranger to her. An elderly woman, with a black silk mantle on her head and over her shoulders, spoke to her. She did not understand the meaning, but she knew the words were Spanish. Then the tide of recollection rushed back, and the black cold night came fully before her, which was the last thing she recollected. 'My father,' she said, rising as well as she could. The woman had gone to the window and beckoned, and in another minute Mr. Ferroll stood by her bedside. 'Can you still love me, Janet?' said he. 'Love you! oh yes, my father.'"

It seems a pity that a concluding chapter was afterwards added, containing a description of Janet's life with her father in Boston, and of his dying moments and last words, which might well have been left to the imagi-

By ADELINE SERGEANT

nation. The original conclusion was more impressive without these details.

It is rather curious, too, that Mrs. Clive should have written another volume to explain *why* Paul Ferroll killed his wife; but possibly she thought further explanation was necessary, since she prefixed to the latter volume a quotation from Froude's "Henry the Eighth": "A man does not murder his wife gratuitously." In this book she changes the names of all the characters except that of Ellinor. Paul Ferroll is Leslie, and his wife, Anne, is Laura. Ellinor, the young and beautiful girl out of a convent, completely enchants Leslie, whom Laura had intended to marry; and Laura contrives, by deliberate malice, so completely to sever them that he makes Laura his wife, while Ellinor returns to the convent. "Violent were the passions of the strong but bitter man; fierce the hatred of the powerful but baffled intellect. Wild was the fury of the man who believed in but one world of good, and saw the mortal moments pass away unenjoyed and irretrievable. Out of these hours arose a purpose. The reader sees the man and knows the deed. From the premises laid before him, he need not indeed conclude that even that man would do the deed, but since it was told in 1855 that the husband killed his wife, so now in 1860 it is explained *why* he killed her."

MRS. ARCHER CLIVE

This second volume is decidedly inferior to the first, but it shared in the popularity which "Paul Ferroll" had already achieved, and the author's vigorous portraiture of characters and events was well marked in both volumes.

With her third volume, "John Greswold," came a sudden falling off, at any rate as regards dramatic force. "John Greswold" is the autobiography of a young man who has very little story to tell and does not know how to tell it. No grip is laid on the reader's attention; no character claims especial interest, but the thing that is remarkable in the book is the literary touch, which is far more perceptible than in the more interesting story of "Paul Ferroll." The book is somewhat inchoate, but contains short passages of real beauty, keen shafts of observation, and an occasional flight of emotional expression, which raise the writer to a greater literary elevation than the merely sensational incidents of her earlier novels. She has gained in reflective power, but lost her dramatic instinct. Consequently "John Greswold" was less successful than "Paul Ferroll."

The conclusion of the book, vague and indecisive, shows the author to be marked out by nature as one of the Impressionist School. It is powerful and yet indefinite; in fact it could only have been written by one with a true poetic gift. "The seven stars that never set are going westward. The funeral car of Lazarus moves on and the three mourners follow behind. They are above the fir wood and that's the sign of midnight. Twenty-three years ago I was born into this world and now the twenty-third has run out. The time is gone. The known things are all over and buried in the darkness behind. Before me lies the great blank page of the future and no writing traced upon it. But it is nothing to me. I won't ask nor think, nor hope, nor fear about it. The leaf of the book is turned and there's an end—the tale is told."

"Paul Ferroll" may be considered as the precursor of the purely sensational novel, or of what may be called the novel of mystery. Miss Brontë in "Jane Eyre" uses to some extent the same kind of material, but her work is far more a study of character than the story of "Paul Ferroll" can claim to be. In "Paul Ferroll," indeed, the analysis of motive is entirely absent. The motives that actuated Paul Ferroll are to be gathered simply from chance expressions or his actions. No description of the human heart has been attempted. The picture of the violent, revengeful, strongly passionate nature of the man is forcible enough, but it is displayed by action and not by introspection. It is for this reason that Mrs. Clive may be placed in the forefront of the sensational novelists of the century. She anticipated the work of Wilkie Collins, of Charles Reade, of Miss Braddon, and many others of their school, in showing human nature as expressed by its energies, neither diagnosing it like a physician, nor analysing it like a priest. A vigorous representation of the outside semblance of things is the peculiar characteristic of the so-called sensational novelist; and it is in this respect that "Paul Ferroll" excels many of the novels of incident written during the first half of this century. It heralded a new departure in the ways of fiction. It set forth the delights of a mystery, the pleasures of suspense, together with a thrilling picture of "the strong man in adversity," which has been beloved of fiction-mongers from the first days of fable in the land.

But perhaps it was successful, most of all, because it introduced its readers to a new sensation. Hitherto they had been taught to look on the hero of a novel as necessarily a noble and virtuous being, endowed with heroic, not to say angelic qualities; but this conviction was now to be reversed. The change was undoubtedly startling. Even Scott had not got beyond the tradition of a good young man as hero, a tradition which the Brontës and Mrs. Archer Clive were destined to break down. For Scott's most fascinating character, Brian de Bois-Guilbert, was confessedly the villain of the piece; and the splendidly picturesque figure of Dundee was supposed to be less attractive than the tame and scrupulous personality of Henry Morton. It was a convention amongst writers that vice and crime must be repulsive, and that there was something inherently attractive in virtue—a wholesome doctrine, insufficiently preached in these days, but not strictly consistent with facts. To find, therefore, a villain—and a thorough-paced villain, the murderer of his wife—installed in the place of hero and represented as noble, handsome, and gifted, naturally thrilled the readers' minds with a mixture of horror and delight. The substitution of villain for hero is now too common to excite remark, but it was a striking event in the days when "Paul Ferroll" was published, although there had been instances of a similar kind in the novels of the eighteenth century. The new fashion gained ground and speedily exceeded the limits which Mrs. Archer Clive would no doubt have set to it; but it is nevertheless in part to her that we owe this curious transposition of *rôles*, which has revolutionised the aims and objects of fiction in the latter half of the nineteenth century.

MRS. HENRY WOOD

THE art of the *raconteur*, pure and simple, is apt to be undervalued in our days. A rage for character-painting, for analysis, for subtle discrimination, down to the minutest detail, has taken hold upon us; and although we have lately returned to a taste for adventure of the more stirring kind, there is still an underlying conviction that the highest forms of literary art deal with mental states and degrees of emotions, instead of with the ordinary complications of everyday life. Hence the person who is gifted simply with a desire (and the power) of telling a story *as* a story, with no ulterior motive, with no ambition of intellectual achievement, the Scheherazade of our quiet evenings and holiday afternoons, is apt to take a much lower place in our estimation than she deserves.

This is especially the case with Mrs. Henry Wood. It is impossible to claim for her any lofty literary position; she is emphatically un-literary and middle-class. But she never has cause to say, "Story? God bless you, I have none to tell, Sir," for she always has a very distinct and convincing story, which she handles with a skill which can perhaps be valued only by the professional novelist, who knows the technical difficulty of handling the numerous *groups* of

By ADELINE SERGEANT

characters which Mrs. Wood especially affects. There is no book of hers which deals—as so many novels deal—with merely one or two characters. She takes the whole town into her story, wherever it may be. We not only know the Lord-Lieutenant and the High Sheriff and the Squire, but we are intimate (particularly intimate) with the families of the local lawyer and doctor. We are almost equally well acquainted with their bootmaker and greengrocer, while their maids and their grooms are as much living entities to us as if they had served us in our own houses. To take a great group of *dramatis personæ*, widely differing in circumstances, in character, in individuality; to keep them all perfectly clear without confusion and without wavering; to evolve from them some central figures on which the attention of the subsidiary characters shall be unavoidably fixed, and to weave a plot of mystery, intrigue, treachery or passion which must be resolved to its ultimate elements before the last page of the book—to do all this is really an achievement of which many a writer, who values himself on his intellectual superiority to Mrs. Henry Wood, might well be proud. It is no more easy to marshal a multitude of characters in the pages of your book than to dispose bodies of soldiers in advantageous positions over an unknown country. The eye of a general is in some respects needed for both opera-

MRS. HENRY WOOD

tions, and the true balance and proportion of a plot are not matters which come by accident or can be accomplished without skill. It may not be literary skill, but it is skill of a kind which deserves recognition, under what name soever it may be classed.

Mrs. Henry Wood was born in Worcestershire in 1814, and died in London in 1887. She suffered from delicate health and passed the greater part of her life as an invalid. She was the daughter of Mr. Thomas Price, one of the largest glove manufacturers in the city of Worcester. She married Mr. Henry Wood, the head of a large banking and shipping firm, who retired early from work and died comparatively young. It was not until middle life that Mrs. Wood began to write; and her first work, —perhaps, of all her works, the most popular—was "East Lynne," which first appeared in *Colburn's New Monthly Magazine*. Its success was prodigious and it is still one of the most popular novels upon the shelves of every circulating library. It has been translated into many languages and dramatised in different forms. It was published in 1861, and reached a fifth edition within the year.

Amongst her most popular works also are "The Channings" and "Mrs. Halliburton's Troubles," 1862; "The Shadow of Ashlydyat," 1863; "St. Martin's Eve," 1866;

By ADELINE SERGEANT

"A Life's Secret," 1867; "Roland Yorke," a sequel to "The Channings," 1869; "Johnny Ludlow," stories reprinted from the *Argosy*, 1874 to 1885; "Edina," 1876; "Pomeroy Abbey," 1878; "Court Netherleigh," 1881; and many other stories and novels. Mrs. Wood was for many years the editor of the *Argosy*.

The reason of the popularity of "East Lynne" is not far to seek. It is, to begin with, a very touching story; and its central situation, which in some respects recalls the relation of the two women in Mrs. Crowe's "Linny Lockwood," is genuinely striking. It is perhaps not worth while to argue as to its probability. It is, of course, barely possible that a woman should come disguised into the house where she formerly reigned as mistress, and act as governess to her own children, without being recognised. As a matter of fact, she is recognised by one of the servants only on account of a momentary forgetfulness of her disguise. Her own husband, her own children, do not know her in the least; and although he and his kinswoman are vaguely troubled by what they consider a chance resemblance, they dismiss it from their minds as utterly impossible, until the day when Lady Isabel, dying in her husband's house, begs to see him for the last time. The changes in her personal appearance, her lameness, for instance, and the greyness of her hair, are very ingeniously contrived; but it certainly seems almost impossible that two or three years should have so completely changed her that nobody should even guess at her identity.

The present generation complains that the pathos of the story is overdone; but even if detail after detail is multiplied, so as to harrow the reader's feelings almost unnecessarily, the fact still remains that Mrs. Wood has imagined as pitiful and tragic a situation as could possibly exist in the domestic relations of man and woman. The erring wife returning to find her husband married to another woman, to nurse one of her own children through his last illness without being recognised by him or by her husband, and to die at last in her husband's house with the merest shadow of consolation in the shape of his somewhat grudging forgiveness, presents us with a figure which cannot fail to be extremely pathetic.

The faults of Mrs. Henry Wood's style, its occasional prolixity and commonplaceness, the iteration of the moral reflections, as well as the triteness and feebleness sometimes of the dialogue, very nearly disappear from view when we resign ourselves to a consideration of this tragic situation. It cannot be denied that there is just a touch of mawkishness now and then, just a slight ring of false sentiment in the pity accorded to Lady Isabel, who was certainly one of the silliest young women that ever existed in the realms of fiction. Nevertheless the spectacle of the mother nursing the dying boy, who does not know her, is one that will always appeal to the heart of the ordinary reader, and will go far to account for the extraordinary popularity of "East Lynne."

A novelist of more aspiring genius would perhaps have concentrated our attention exclusively upon Lady Isabel's feelings and tragic fate. Here Mrs. Wood's failings, as well as her capacities, reveal themselves. She sees the tragic side of things, but she sees also (and perhaps too much) the pathos of small incidents, the importance of trifles. She spares us no jot of the sordid side of life. And in a novel of the undoubted power of "East Lynne" there are some details which might have been spared us. The rapacity of the creditors who seize the body of Lady Isabel's father, the gossip of the servants, the suspicions of Afy Hallijohn, and, in short, almost all the underplot respecting Richard Hare—these matters are superfluous. The reader's eye ought to be kept more attentively upon the heroine and her relations with Mr. Carlisle and Sir Francis. The one inexplicable point in the story is Lady Isabel's desertion of her husband for a man whom she must despise. It is never hinted that she had for one moment lost her heart to Francis Levison. She left her husband out of sheer pique and jealousy, loving him ardently all the while, although, in her ignorance and folly, she scarcely knew that she loved him. Here the story is weak. We feel that Mrs. Wood sacrifices probability in her effort to obtain a striking situation. For the strongest part of " East Lynne " is the description of what occurs when Lady Isabel returns as a governess to her old home, when her husband, supposing her to be dead, has married his old love Barbara Hare. To this situation, everything is subordinate ; and it is in itself so strong that we cannot wonder if the author strains a point or two in order to achieve it.

But the curious, the characteristic, thing is that even in this supreme crisis of the story, Mrs. Wood's essential love of detail, and of somewhat commonplace detail, asserts itself over and over again. The incidents she takes pains to narrate are rational enough. There is no reason why pathos should be marred because a dying child asks for cheese with his tea, or because the sensible stepmother condemns Lucy to a diet of bread and water for some trifling offence, or because Miss Cornelia Carlisle displays her laughable eccentricities at Lady Isabel's bedside. The pathos is marred now and then, not because of these trifling yet irritating incidents, but because we get an

By ADELINE SERGEANT

impression that the author has forced a number of utterly prosaic people into a tragic situation for which they are eminently unfitted. The ducking of Sir Francis Levison in the horsepond is an example of this. The man was a heartless villain and murderer, yet he is presented to us in a scene of almost vulgar farce as part of his retribution. If the author had herself realised the insufficiency of her characters to rise to the tragic height demanded of them, she might have achieved either satire or intense realism; but there is a certain smugness in Mrs. Henry Wood's acceptance of the commonplaces of life which makes us feel her an inadequate painter of tragedy. We close the book with a suspicion that she preferred the intolerable Barbara to the winsome and erring Lady Isabel.

"East Lynne" owes half its popularity, however, to that reaction against inane and impossible goodness which has taken place since the middle of the century. Just as Rochester and Paul Ferroll are protests against the conventional hero, so Lady Isabel is a protest against the conventional heroine—and a portent of her time! We were all familiar with beauty and virtue in distress, from Clarissa Harlowe downwards. It is during later years that we have become conversant with beauty and guilt as objects of our sympathy and commiseration.

MRS. HENRY WOOD

The moralists of the time—Saturday Reviewers, and others—perceived the change from one point of view, and were not slow to comment on it. Their opposition to the modern novel was chiefly based upon what they called a glorification of vice and crime. Now that the mists of prejudice have cleared away, we can see very well that no more praise of wrongdoing was implied by Mrs. Wood's portrait of Lady Isabel than by Thackeray's keen-edged delineation of Becky Sharp or George Eliot's sorrowful sympathy with Maggie Tulliver. What was at first set down as a new and revolutionary kind of admiration for weakness and criminality soon resolved itself into a manifestation of that remarkable *Zeit-Geist* which has made itself felt in every department of human life. It is that side of the modern spirit which leads to the comprehension of the sufferings of others, to a new pity for their faults and weaknesses, a new breadth of tolerance, and a generous reluctance to judge harshly of one's fellow man. It has crept into the domain of law, of religious thought, of philanthropic effort, and it cannot be excluded from the realms of literature and art. It is, in fact, the scientific spirit, which says "there's nothing good or ill but thinking makes it so;" which refuses to dogmatise or hastily to condemn; which looks for the motives and reasons and causes of men's actions, and knows the infinite gradations between folly and wisdom, between black and white, between right and wrong. If science had done nothing else, it would be an enormous gain that she should teach us to suspend our judgment, to weigh evidence, and thus to pave the way for that diviner spirit by which we refuse to consider any sinner irreclaimable or any criminal beyond the reach of human sympathy.

"East Lynne" was received with general acclamation, and has been translated, it is said, into every known tongue, including Parsee and Hindustanee. "Some years ago," her son states, "one of the chief librarians in Madrid informed Mrs. Henry Wood that the most popular book on his shelves, original or translated, was 'East Lynne.' Not very long ago it was translated into Welsh and brought out in a Welsh newspaper. It has been dramatised and played so often that had the author received a small royalty from every representation it was long since estimated that it would have returned to her no less than a quarter of a million sterling, but she never received anything. . . . . In the English Colonies the sale of the various works increased steadily year by year. In France the story has been dramatised and is frequently played in Paris and the Provinces." On its first appearance, an enthusiastic review in the *Times* produced a tremendous effect upon the public; the libraries were besieged for copies, and the printers had to work night and day upon new editions. In fact the success of "East Lynne" was one of the most remarkable literary incidents of the century.

The most popular of Mrs. Henry Wood's books, next to "East Lynne," seem to be "Mrs. Halliburton's Troubles" and "The Channings." These are stories of more entirely quiet domestic interest than "East Lynne." The situations are less tragical and the plots less complicated. Mrs. Halliburton's quiet endurance of the privations and difficulties of her life, the pathetic life and death of her little Janey, and the ultimate success and achievements of her sons, linger in the memory of the reader as a pleasant and homely picture of the vicissitudes of English life.

There is a more humorous element in " The Channings," from the introduction of so many youthful characters— the boys of the Cathedral school, notably Bywater, who is the incarnation of good-humoured impudence, giving brightness to the tone of the story. The schoolboys are in this, as in many other of Mrs. Wood's novels, particularly well drawn. They are not prigs; they are anything but angels, in spite of their white surplices and their beautiful voices; and their escapades and adventures in

By ADELINE SERGEANT

the old cloisters were wild enough to make the old mon s turn in their graves. No doubt many incidents of this kind were drawn from life and owe their origin to Mrs. Wood's acquaintance with the Choir School belonging to Worcester Cathedral.

It was not the only occasion on which the manufacturer's daughter turned her knowledge of Worcester to good account. It may be said that the majority of her novels are coloured, more or less, by the author's lengthy residence in a cathedral town. It was in 1874 that the first series of short stories, supposed to be narrated by Johnny Ludlow, began in the *Argosy*. Johnny Ludlow is a young lad belonging to a Worcestershire family, who is supposed to narrate incidents which have come under his observation at school or at home. Some of the stories thus produced are striking and vigorous; others are of less merit, but all are distinguished by the strong individuality of the characters, and by the fidelity with which Worcester and Worcestershire life are described. It now seems extraordinary that there should have been the slightest doubt as to the authorship of these stories, for Mrs. Wood's peculiarities of style are observable on every page. Mr. Charles W. Wood, her son, remarks that "no one knew, or even guessed at, the authorship;" but this is a rather exaggerated statement, as we have reason to be aware that the author was recognised at once by critics of discrimination. Still the general public were for some time deceived, imagining Johnny Ludlow to be a new author, whose stories they occasionally contrasted with those of Mrs. Henry Wood, and were said to prefer, probably much to the novelist's own amusement.

The great variety of plot and incident found in the "Johnny Ludlow" stories is their most remarkable feature. The same characters are, of course, introduced again and again, as Johnny Ludlow moves in a circle of country squires, clergy, and townspeople. But it is astonishing with how much effect the stories of different lives can be placed in the same setting, and with what infinite changes the life of a country district can be reproduced. The characters are clearly drawn and often very well contrasted, and no doubt Mrs. Henry Wood's memories of her earlier life in the district contributed largely to the success of this series. The first series ran in the *Argosy* and were re-printed, 1874-1880, while a second and third series maintained their popularity in 1881 and in 1885.

It has been computed that Mrs. Wood wrote not fewer than from three to four hundred short stories, every one of them with a distinct and carefully worked-out plot, in addition to nearly forty long novels : a proof, if any were wanted, of the extreme fertility of her imagination and the facility of her pen.

It has, however, sometimes been wondered why Mrs. Henry Wood's works should have attained so great a circulation when they are conspicuously wanting in the higher graces of literary style or intellectual attainment. The reason appears to lie chiefly in certain qualities of her writings which appeal in an entirely creditable way to the heart and mind of the British public. Mrs. Wood's stories, although sensational in plot, are purely domestic. They are concerned chiefly with the great middle-class of England, and she describes lower middle-class life with a zest and a conviction and a sincerity which we do not find in many modern writers, who are apt to sneer at the *bourgeois* habits and modes of thought found in so many English households. Now the *bourgeoisie* does not like to be sneered at. If it eats tripe and onions, and wears bright blue silk dresses, and rejoices in dinner-tea, it nevertheless considers its fashions to be as well worth serious attention as those of the Upper Ten. Mrs. Henry Wood never satirises, she only records. It is her fidelity to truth, to the smallest domestic detail, which has charmed and will continue to charm, a large circle of readers, who are inclined perhaps to glory in the name of "Philistine."

Then there is the loftier quality of a high, if somewhat conventional, moral tone. Mrs. Wood's novels are emphatically on the side of purity, honesty, domestic life and happiness. There is no book of hers which does not breathe this spirit, or can be said to be anything but harmless. Her character-drawing has merit; but it is not to be wondered at, considering the number of works she produced, that she should repeat the same type over and over again with a certain monotonous effect. The sweet and gentle wife and mother, not too strong in character, but perfectly refined and conscientious, such as Maria in the "Shadow of Ashlydyat"; the "perfect gentleman," noble, upright, proud, generally with blue eyes and straight features, like Oswald Cray and Mr. Carlisle and Mr. North—these are characters with which we continually meet and of which, admirable in themselves as they are, we sometimes weary. But although the portraiture is not very subtle, it is on the whole faithful to life.

Then there is that especial group of Mrs. Wood's stories already mentioned, into which an element of freshness, then somewhat unusual in fiction, is largely introduced. These are the stories which have much to do with boys and

By ADELINE SERGEANT

boy-life—notably "The Channings," "Roland Yorke," "Orville College," "Mrs. Halliburton's Troubles," "Lady Grace," and the "Johnny Ludlow" series. These books, less sensational in plot than many of Mrs. Wood's novels, have been peculiarly successful, perhaps because the scenes and characters are largely drawn from real life. Mrs. Wood's long residence at Worcester made her familiar with the life of the college boys, who haunt the precincts of the stately old cathedral, and she has introduced her knowledge of their pranks with very great effect. Her descriptions of the old city itself, of the streets, of the cloisters, of the outlying villages and byways, are remarkably accurate, and remind one of the use which Charles Dickens made, in the same way, of Rochester and its cathedral.

It is really extraordinary to see how large a part of Mrs. Wood's work is concerned with Worcester, and how well she could render, when she chose, the dialogue of the country and the customs of its people. The reason is, of course, that these things are true; that she gives us in these books a part of her own experience, of her own life. Another group of her books is interesting for a similar reason—the novels in which she deals with business life, and the relations of employers to their men. Such are "A Life's Secret," which is the very interesting history of

MRS. HENRY WOOD

a strike; "The Foggy Night at Offord," "Mrs. Halliburton's Troubles," and several of the "Johnny Ludlow" stories, where incidents of the manufacturing districts of England have been introduced with very good effect, Mrs. Wood's own connection with glove manufacturers in Worcester having supplied her with ample materials for this kind of fiction. In "A Life's Secret" there is an extremely clever picture of the lower type of workman, and some excellent sketches of poor people and of the misery they suffer during the strike and subsequent lockout.

The third class of Mrs. Wood's books consists of what may be called works of pure imagination, with sometimes a slight touch of the romantic and supernatural—such as "The Shadow of Ashlydyat," "St. Martin's Eve," "Lady Adelaide's Oath," "Lord Oakburn's Daughters," "George Canterbury's Will," etc. From the literary point of view these books are less worthy than the others, but they are particularly well constructed and ingenious. There are no loose ends, and Mrs. Wood's skill in weaving a plot seems never to have diminished to the last day of her life. But her earlier and perhaps simpler work had more real value than even the books which display such great constructive skill. Mrs. Wood would possibly have taken a higher place amongst English novelists if she had avoided mere sensation, and confined herself to what she could do well—namely, the faithful and realistic rendering of English middle class life. She has had, perhaps, more popularity than any novelist of the Victorian age; and her popularity is justified by the wholesomeness and purity of her moral tone, the ingenuity and sustained interest of her plots, and the quiet truthfulness, in many cases, of her delineation of character.

Her faults are those of the class for which she wrote, her merits are theirs also. It is no small praise to say that she never revelled in dangerous situations, nor justified the wrong-doing of any of her characters. When one considers the amount of work that she produced, and the nature of that work, it is amazing to reflect on the variety of incident and character which she managed to secure. Her plots often turned upon sad or even tragic events, but the sadness and the tragedy were natural and simple. There was nothing unwholesome about her books. She will probably be read and remembered longer than many writers of a far higher literary standing; and although fashions, even in fiction, have greatly changed since the days when "East Lynne" and "The Channings" made their mark, there is no doubt that they hold their place in the affections of many an English novel-reader. They neither aim high nor fall low: their gentle mediocrity

MRS. HENRY WOOD

is soothing; and they are not without those gleams of insight and intensity which reveal the gift of the born story-teller—a title to which Mrs. Henry Wood may well lay claim.

Adeline Sergeant.

LADY GEORGIANA FULLERTON MRS. STRETTON. ANNE MANNING

By CHARLOTTE M. YONGE

LADY GEORGIANA FULLERTON MRS. STRETTON. ANNE MANNING

THE three ladies here grouped together are similar in the purity and principle which breathe throughout their writings, though different in other respects. The first named wrote in the stress, and later in the calm, of a religious struggle; the second in the peaceful, fond memory of a happy home-life; the third in the pleasurable realisation of historic days long gone by. In each case, the life is reflected in the books.

GEORGIANA CHARLOTTE LEVESON GOWER was born on September 23, 1812, being the second daughter of one of those noble families predestined, by their rank and condition, to a diplomatic course. Her father became ultimately Earl Granville, and when his little daughter was twelve years old, he received the appointment of ambassador at Paris. It is well known that the upper diplomatic circles form the *crème de la crème* of aristocratic society, their breeding, refinement, knowledge of man and manners, as well as their tact, being almost necessarily of the highest order. Lady Granville was noted for her admirable management of her receptions, and her power of steering her way through the motley crowd of visitors and residents presented to her. The charm of her manner was very remarkable, and made a great impression on all who came in her way. And, giving reality and absolute sincerity to all this unfailing sweetness, Lady Granville was a deeply religious and conscientious woman, who trained her daughters to the highest standard of excellence, and taught them earnest devotion.

Naturally, French was as familiar to the young ladies as English, and they became intimate with many of the best and purest families in France, among others, with that of de Ferronaye, whose memoirs, as told by one of them, Mrs. Augustus Craven, has touched many hearts. It was a happy life, in which study and accomplishment had their place, and gaieties did not lose the zest of youthful enjoyment because they were part of the duty of station.

By CHARLOTTE M. YONGE

Between France and England the time of the family was spent, and, in 1833, both sisters were married—Lady Georgiana on July 13, to Alexander Fullerton, heir to considerable estates in Gloucestershire and in Ireland. He had been in the Guards, but had resigned his commission, and become an *attaché* to the Embassy at Paris. There the young couple continued, and there, at the end of the year, was born their only child, a son, whose very delicate health was a constant anxiety.

In 1841 Lord Granville ceased to be ambassador, and the whole family led a wandering life in the South of France, Italy, and Germany, interspersed with visits in England. In 1843 Mr. Fullerton, after long study of the controversy, was received into the Church of Rome. His wife had always greatly delighted in the deep and beautiful rites of that communion, in its best aspects, and many of her most intimate friends were devout and enlightened members of that Church ; but she had been bred up as a faithful Anglican, and she made no change as long as her father lived. The tale on which her chief fame rests was the product of the heart-searchings that she underwent, at the very time when the thoughts and studies of good men were tending to discover neglected truths in the Church of England.

LADY GEORGIANA FULLERTON

Lady Georgiana said, in her old age, that she had never written for her own pleasure, or to find expression of feeling, but always with a view to the gains for her charities. She would rather have written poetry, and the first impulse was given by her publisher telling her that she would find a novel far more profitable than verses. Yet it is hardly possible to believe that when once embarked she did not write from her heart. She was a long time at work on her tale, which was written during sojourns at various continental resorts, and finally submitted to two such different critics as Lord Brougham and Charles Greville, both of whom were carried away by admiration of the wonderful pathos of the narrative, and the charm of description, as well as the character-drawing. It is, however, curious that, while marking some lesser mistakes, neither advised her to avoid the difficulty which makes the entire plot an impossibility, namely, the omission of an inquest, which must have rendered the secrecy of "Ellen Middleton" out of the question.

The story opens most effectively with the appearance of a worn and wasted worshipper in Salisbury Cathedral. One of the canons becomes interested, and with much difficulty induces her to confide her griefs to him in an autobiography, which she had intended to be read only after her death. The keynote of Ellen's misfortunes is a

By CHARLOTTE M. YONGE

slight blow, given in a moment of temper, at fifteen years old, to her cousin, a naughty child of eight, causing a fatal fall into the river below. No one knows the manner of the disaster, except two persons whose presence was unknown to her: Henry Lovell, a relative of the family, and his old nurse, whom he swears to silence.

This woman, however, cannot refrain from strewing mysterious hints in Ellen's way, and Henry Lovell obtains a power over the poor girl which is the bane of her life. His old nurse (by very unlikely means) drives him into a marriage with her grand-daughter, Alice, whose lovely, innocent, devotional character, is one of the great charms of the book. Ellen, almost at the same time, marries her cousin, Edward Middleton, whom she loves with all her heart; but he is a hard man, severe in his integrity, and his distrust is awakened by Henry's real love for Ellen, and the machinations by which he tries to protect her from the malice of the old nurse. The net closes nearer and nearer round Ellen, till at last Edward finds her on her knees before Henry, conjuring him to let her confess her secret. Without giving her a hearing, Edward commands her to quit his house. A letter from Henry, declaring that she is his own, and that she will not escape him, drives her to seek concealment at Salisbury, where she is dying of consumption, caused by her broken heart, when the good canon finds her, gives her absolution, and brings about repentance, reconciliation, and an infinite peace, in which we are well content to let her pass away, tended by her husband, her mother-like aunt, and the gentle Alice.

It is altogether a fine tragedy. The strong passions of Henry Lovell, the enthusiastic nature of Ellen, beaten back in every higher flight by recurring threats from her enemies, the unbending nature of Edward, and in the midst the exquisite sweetness of Alice, like a dove in the midst of the tempest, won all hearts, either by the masterly analysis of passion or by the beauty of delineation, while the religious side of the tale was warmly welcomed by those who did not think, like Lord Brougham, that it was "rank Popery." The sense of the power and beauty of the story is only enhanced by freshly reading it after the lapse of many years.

Naturally, it was a great success, and the second book, "Grantley Manor," which was not published till after her father's death and her own secession to Rome, was floated up on the same tide of popularity. It contrasted two half-sisters, Margaret and Ginevra, one wholly English, the other half Italian by race and entirely so by breeding. Still, though Ginevra is the more fascinating, Margaret is her superior in straightforward truth. For, indeed, Lady

By CHARLOTTE M. YONGE

Georgiana never fell into the too frequent evil of depreciation and contempt of the system she had quitted, and remained open-minded and loving to the last. The excellence of style and knowledge of character as well as the tone of high breeding which are felt in all these writings recommended both this and "Ladybird," published in 1852. Both are far above the level of the ordinary novel, and some readers preferred "Ladybird" to the two predecessors.

In the meantime, an estate in England at Midgham had become a home, and young Granville Fullerton had gone into the army. On the 29th of May 1855, he was cut off by a sudden illness, and his parents' life was ever after a maimed one, though full of submission and devotion. Externally, indeed, Lady Georgiana still showed her bright playfulness of manner, and keen interest in all around her, so that the charm of her society was very great, but her soul was the more entirely absorbed in religion and in charity, doing the most menial offices for the sick poor and throwing herself into the pleasures of little children. She questioned with herself whether she ought to spend time in writing instead of on her poor, when the former task meant earning two hundred pounds a year for them, but she decided on uniting the two occupations, the more readily because she found that her works had a good influence and helped on a religious serial in which she took a warm interest.

But her *motifs* were now taken from history, not actual life. "La Comtesse de Boneval" is a really marvellous *tour de force*, being a development from a few actual letters written by a poor young wife, whose reluctant husband left her, after ten days, for foreign service, and never returned. Lady Georgiana makes clear the child's hero-worship, the brief gleam of gladness, the brave resolve not to interfere with duty and honour, and the dreary deserted condition. All is written in French, not only pure and grammatical, but giving in a wonderful manner the epigrammatic life and freshness of the old Parisian society. This is really the ablest, perhaps the most pathetic, of her books.

"Ann Sherwood" is a picture of the sufferings of the Romanists in Elizabethan times, "A Stormy Life" is the narrative of a companion of Margaret of Anjou—both showing too much of the author's bias. "Too Strange not to be True" is founded on a very curious story, disinterred by Lord Dover, purporting that the unhappy German wife of the ferociously insane son of Peter the Great, at the point of death from his brutality, was smuggled away by her servants, with the help of Countess

By CHARLOTTE M. YONGE

Konigsmark, the mother of Marshal Saxe, while a false funeral took place. She was conveyed to the French Settlements in Louisiana, and there, after hearing that the Czarowitz was dead, she married a French gentleman, the Chevalier d'Auban. Here, in these days of one-volume tales, the story might well have ended, but Lady Georgiana pursues the history through the latter days of the princess, after she had returned to Europe and had been bereaved of her husband and her daughter. She lived at Brussels, and again met Marshal Saxe in her extreme old age. The figures of the Chevalier, and the sweet daughter, Mina, are very winning and graceful, and there are some most interesting descriptions of the Jesuit missions to the Red Indians; but, as a whole, the book had better have closed with the marriage with d'Auban.

There is little more to say of Lady Georgiana's life. It was always affectionate, cheerful and unselfish, and it became increasingly devout as she grew older. After a long illness, she died at Bournemouth, on the 19th of January 1885, remembered fondly by many, and honoured by all who knew her saintly life. As to literary fame, she may be described as having written one first-rate book and a number fairly above the average.

MRS. STRETTON

ABOUT the same time as "Ellen Middleton" appeared, a novel was making its way rather by force of affectionate family portraiture than by plot or incident. "The Valley of a Hundred Fires" is really and truly Mrs. Stretton's picture of her father and mother, and her home; and her mother is altogether her heroine, while old family habits and anecdotes are given with only a few alterations. "The Valley of the Hundred Fires" has been placed by her on the borders of Wales, but it really was Gateshead, in Durham, quite as black and quite as grimy as the more southern region, inasmuch as no flowers would grow in the Rectory garden which, nevertheless, the children loved so heartily as to call it dear old Dingy. (It is Cinder Tip in the story.) Literally, they lived so as to show that

> "Love's a flower that will not die
> For lack of leafy screen;
> And Christian hope may cheer the eye
> That ne'er saw vernal green;"

and that—at least, in the early days of this century—an abnormally large family was no misfortune to themselves or their parents.

By CHARLOTTE M. YONGE

The real name was Collinson, and the deep goodness and beneficence of the father, the Reverend John Collinson, and the undaunted cheerfulness, motherliness, and discipline of Emily, his wife, shine throughout, not at all idealised. The number of their children was fifteen, ten daughters and five sons; and the second daughter, Julia Cecilia, was, as she describes herself, a tall, lank, yellow baby who was born on the 25th of November 1812. She became as the eldest daughter to the others, for there had always been a promise that if there were several girls the eldest should be adopted by her aunt, wife to a clergyman and childless.

The two homes were a great contrast: the one kept in absolute order and great refinement, with music and flowers the constant delight and occupation, and the single adopted child trained up in all the precision of the household; while the other was a house of joyous freedom, kept under the needful restraints of sound religious principle, discipline and unselfishness. The story went that when the children were asked how many of them there were, they answered, "One young lady and eight little girls." Mrs. Collinson used to say, that if she ever saw any signs that her "one young lady" was either pining for companionship, or growing spoilt by the position, she would recall her at once; but the child was always happy and obedient, and pleased to impart her accomplishments to her sisters, who admired without jealousy. Comical adventures are recorded in the "Valley," such as when the whole train of little damsels, walking out under the convoy of Julia and a young nurserymaid, encountered a bull, which had lifted a gate on its horns. The maid thrust the baby into Julia's arms and ran away, while her charges retired into a ditch, the elder ones not much alarmed, because, as they said, the bull could not hurt them with the gate on its horns. It passed safely by them; but the little ones confessed to having been dreadfully frightened by a snail in the ditch, "which put out its horns like a little Kerry cow," and it creeped and it creeped!

One incident in their early childhood was the rioting that pervaded the collieries in the years immediately following the great French war. Mr. Collinson, being a magistrate, was called upon to accompany the dragoons in order to read the Riot Act. He thus left his family unprotected; but the seven thousand pitmen never touched the Rectory, and, according to the "Valley," replied courteously to two of the children, who rushed out to the top of the Cinder Tip, begging to know whether they had seen "our papa" and if he was safe.

There was another sadder episode, related also with much feeling, though a little altered, for it concerned the

By CHARLOTTE M. YONGE

second son, not the eldest (then the only son) as described. A blow from a cricket ball did irreparable mischief to his knee, and it was suddenly decreed that amputation was necessary, long before the days of chloroform. The father was away from home, the mother sentenced not to be present, and the doctors consented that Julia should hold the patient's hand, smooth his hair, and try to tell him stories through the operation. It was successfully and bravely carried out, but the evil was not removed, and a few weeks later this much-loved boy was taken away. The circumstances, very beautiful and consoling, are given in the story; and there too is told how, before sunset on that sad day, the ninth little daughter was given, and struggled hard for the vigorous life she afterwards attained.

The "Parson's man" said one day, when his mistress, for once in her life, indulged in a sigh that her garden could never rival that of her sister, "We've got the finer flowers, ma'am."

Education was not the tyrannical care in those days that it is at present, and the young people obtained it partly through their parents, some at school, and some by the help of their grandmother and their aunt, but mostly by their own intelligence and exertions; and the family income was augmented by Mr. Collinson taking pupils.

MRS. STRETTON

He had a fair private income; he had a curate, and was able to give a good education to his sons, one of whom made himself a name as Admiral Collinson, one of the Arctic explorers. If there were anxieties, they did not tell upon the children, whose memories reflect little save sunshine.

At nineteen, Julia Collinson became the wife of Walter de Winton, Esquire, of Maedlwch Castle, Radnorshire; but after only twelve years was left a widow, with two sons and a daughter. Her life was devoted to making their home as bright and joyous as her own had been; and it was only in the loneliness that ensued on the children going to school that her authorship commenced, with a child's book called "The Lonely Island."

Later she wrote "The Valley of the Hundred Fires," tracing the habits, characters and the destiny of the family of Gateshead. The father was by this time dead, and extracts from his sermons and diary appear; but "Emily," the mother, is the real heroine of the whole narrative, and though there is so little plot that it hardly deserves the name of novel, there is a wonderful charm in the delineation. There are a few descriptions of manners and of dresses which are amusing; nor must we omit the portrait of the grandmother, Mrs. King (called Reine in the

By CHARLOTTE M. YONGE

book), daughter to the governor of one of the colonies in America before the separation, with the manners of her former princess-ship and something of the despotism. She was a friend of Hannah More, a beneficent builder of schools, and produced a revolt by herself cutting the hair of all the scholars!

"The Queen of the County" relates Mrs. de Winton's experiences of elections among "the stormy hills of Wales" in the early days of the Reform Bill. "Margaret and her Bridesmaids" draws more upon invention. Each of two young girls, through the injudiciousness of her parents, has married the *wrong* person. Margaret acquiesces too much in her husband's indolence, and when herself roused to the perception of duty tries in vain to recover lost ground. Her friend Lottie is a high-spirited little soul, determined to do her duty as a wife, but not to pretend the love she does not feel, till it has been won. She is rather provokingly and unnaturally perfect, especially as she is only seventeen, always knowing when to obey up to the letter in a manner which must so have "riled" her husband that his persistent love is hardly credible, though it shows itself in attempts to isolate her, so that she shall have no resource save himself. His endeavours bring upon him heart complaint, whereof he dies, under her tender care, though she never affects to be

MRS. STRETTON

grief-stricken. Only, as Margaret has lost her husband about the same time in a yachting accident, Lottie refuses to listen to the addresses of a former lover of Margaret's until she is convinced both that her friend will never form another attachment and that the original passion she had inspired is absolutely dead. There is a good deal of character in the story, though overdrawn, and it has survived so as to call for a new edition.

To her children, as well as to her many nephews and nieces, Mrs. de Winton was a charming companion-mother, always fresh, young, vigorous and as full of playfulness as the Julia who led the band of little sisters. When all her children were grown up, in 1858, she married Richard William Stretton, who had been their guardian and an intimate friend of the family, by whom he was much beloved. He died in 1868, and Mrs. Stretton followed him on the 17th of July 1878, leaving behind her one of the brightest of memories. Her books are emphatically herself in their liveliness, their tenderness, their fond enshrining of the past.

By CHARLOTTE M. YONGE

THE third of our group had an even more eventless life, and, instead of letting her imagination dwell on her own past, she studied the women of past history, and realised what they must have felt and thought in the scenes where most of them figure only as names. Her father belonged to the higher professional class, and lived with his large family, of whom Anne was the eldest, at the Paragon, Chelsea, where at eight years old Anne listened to the crash of the carriages, when the Bourbons were on their return to France, and witnessed the ecstasy of London on the visit of the Allied Sovereigns after Waterloo.

With the help of masters for special accomplishments, the daughters had the best of educations, namely, the stimulating influence of their father, an accomplished man, for whom they practised their music, wrote their themes, went out star-gazing, and studied astronomy, listening with delight to his admirable reading of Scott or Shakspere; they also had the absolute freedom of an extensive library. Anne Manning was pronounced to be no genius, but a most diligent, industrious girl; as indeed was proved, for, becoming convinced during the brief reign of a good governess of the duty of solid reading, she voluntarily read from the age of fourteen ten pages a day of real, if dry, history, persevering year after year, and thus unconsciously laying in a good foundation for her future work.

For health's sake the family went into the country, where they became tenants of a tumble-down Cistercian priory on the borders of Salisbury Plain. The numerous girls, with their mother and governess, lived there constantly; the father coming down as often as his business would allow, almost always by the Saturday coach, to spend Sunday. Here the first literary venture was made, when Anne was about seventeen. It was a short dialogue on a serious subject, which a young aunt managed to get accepted in St. Paul's Churchyard; and, as Miss Manning candidly avows, was so well advertised privately by her fond grandfather that—such were the palmy days of authorship—five hundred copies brought her in a profit of £60.

The story, "Village Belles," was completed at Tenby, the Priory having become too ruinous for habitation. It was put into the hands of Baldwin and Cradock, and no proofs were sent till the whole of the two first volumes came together. It was introduced to Mr. Manning thus, "Papa, I don't know what you will say, but I have been writing a story."

"Ho! ho! ho!" was his first answer, but he afterwards said, "My dear, I like your story very much"—and never again referred to it.

Her own after judgment was that it was an "incurably young, inexperienced tale which, after all top dressing, remained but daisied meadow grass."

Sorrow came in to fill the minds of the family (to the exclusion of mere fictitious interests) in the deaths within short intervals of two of the sisters, and their mother's invalidism, ending, within a few years, in her death. After this the winters were spent by the three sisters at the Paragon, the summers in a cottage at Penshurst, their father coming down for the Sunday. Anne Manning, meantime, was pursuing studies in painting and was an excellent amateur artist. She was also a botanist, and this has much to do with her accuracy in writing details of country life and habits.

Dates, alas! are wanting both in her own " Passages in the life of an Authoress," and in the recollections of her kind and affectionate biographer, Mrs. Batty; but it seems to have been in 1849 that her "Maiden and Married Life of Mary Powell," at first written to amuse herself and her sisters, and afterwards sent to assist a brother in Australia, who was starting a local magazine, was given to the editor of "Sharpe's Magazine," then in its early youth.

It made her fame. Nobody had particularly thought of Milton in his domestic capacity before, except as having advocated divorce and made his daughters read Greek to him, and it was reserved for Miss Manning to make the wife paint her own portrait as the lively, eager girl, happy in country freedom with her brothers, important with her "housewife-skep" in her mother's absence, pleased with dress, but touched by the beautiful countenance and the sudden admiration of the strange visitor. There proves to be a debt which makes her marriage with him convenient to the father, and it is carried out in spite of the mother's strong objections, alike to the suitor's age, his politics, and his puritanism. We go along with the country girl in her disappointment and sense of dreariness in her unaccustomed London life, in the staid and serious household, where she sorely misses her brothers and is soon condemned for love of junketing. Then come her joy in her visit to her home at Forest Hill and her reluctance to return, fortified by her father's disapproval of Milton's opinions. By the time that a visit to some wise relatives has brought her to a better mind and to yearning after her husband, Milton has taken offence and has put forth his plea for divorce, which so angers her father that he will not hear of her return; nor does she go back till after many months and the surrender of Oxford, when on her own impulse she hurries to London, meets her husband unexpectedly, and when he "looks down on her with goodness and sweetness 'tis like the sun's gleams shining after rain."

There Mary Powell's journal ends. It is written in beautiful English, such as might well have been contemporary and could only have been acquired by familiarity with the writers of the period, flowing along without effort or pedantry so as to be a really successful imitation. It crept into separate publication anonymously, and achieved a great success, being in fact the first of many books imitating the like style of autobiography; nor has it ever been allowed to drop into oblivion. It was followed up after a time by "Deborah's Diary," being the record supposed to be kept by Milton's one faithful and dutiful daughter, who lived with him in his old age.

The "fascination of the old style," as she calls it, led her to deal with "The Household of Sir Thomas More" in the person of his noble daughter Margaret. There was a good deal more genuine material here, and she has woven in the fragments from Erasmus and others with great ingenuity, and imitated the style of the fifteenth century as well as she had done that of the seventeenth.

ANNE MANNING

From that time Anne Manning's books had a ready sale, though still her name did not appear. "Cherry and Violet" was a tale of the plague of London; "Edward Osborne" told of the apprentice who leapt from the window of a house on London Bridge to save his master's daughter from drowning; "The Old Chelsea Bunhouse" described the haunts with which Miss Manning was familiar; and there were other stories of country life, such as the "Ladies of Bever Hollow." All were written in the purest style, such as could only be attained by one to whom slipshod writing was impossible, and to whom it was equally impossible not to write what was gentle, charitable, and full of religious principle.

Miss Manning was a kind friend and charming letter-writer. Her health began to fail in 1854, when she was writing for a magazine "Some Passages in the Life of an Authoress," never completed. She continued to be an invalid under the care of her sisters till her death on the 14th of September, 1879.

DINAH MULOCK (MRS. CRAIK)

By MRS. PARR

DINAH MULOCK (MRS. CRAIK)

IN the small circle of women writers who shed literary lustre on the early years of her present Majesty's reign was Dinah Mulock, best known to the present novel-reading generation as the author of "John Halifax, Gentleman."

To appreciate fully the position that we claim for her, it will be necessary to turn back to the period when she began to write, and see who were her contemporaries.

Pre-eminent among these stand out three names—names immortal on the roll of fame for so long as taste and critical judgment last; the books of Charlotte Brontë, Elizabeth Gaskell, and George Eliot must be regarded as masterpieces of fiction. We, their humble followers, bow before their genius which time, fashion, or progress cannot dim or take from; therefore, to have achieved success and to have made an abiding fame while such

DINAH MULOCK (MRS. CRAIK)

luminaries were shining in the firmament was a distinction to be justly proud of—the result of talent, delicacy of handling, and grasp of character that were only a little below genius.

How vast the difference that one small step would have made it is not our purpose to show; our intention is rather to take a general view of the work of a writer who—now that close upon half a century has passed, since, in 1849, timidly and without giving her name, she launched on the world her first novel, "The Ogilvies"—has never lost her hold upon the reading public of Great Britain, the Colonies, America, or wherever the English tongue is spoken.

Dinah Mulock was born in 1826 at Stoke-upon-Trent in Staffordshire. Her disposition towards literature seems to have been inherited from her father, who was connected—but in no very prosperous way—with letters, and was known to Byron and to the poet Moore, whose fellow countryman he was. At the time of his daughter's birth, he was acting as spiritual minister to a small congregation who were followers of what were then generally thought to be his advanced and unorthodox opinions. Few who forsake the established road for their own peculiar rut find that prosperity bears them company, and the fortunes of

By MRS. PARR

the Mulock family during the embryo authoress's early years were unsettled and unsatisfactory. We are all given to rebel against the clouds which overcast our youth, seldom realising that to this pinch of adverse circumstance we owe much of that power to depict the sorrows, joys, and perplexities of life in the setting forth of which Miss Mulock became so eminently successful.

Before she had reached the age of twenty, she left her home and came to London, "feeling conscious," we are told, "of a vocation for authorship."

Now, in the present day, when novel writing has become an employment, profession, distraction, I might almost say a curse, there would be nothing remarkable in such a conviction ; but in 1846 the mania of desiring to see their names in print had not seized upon our sex ; therefore the divine afflatus must have been very strong which sent a timid attractive girl, hampered by all the prejudices of her day, to try the fortunes of her pen in London.

That she had not been deceived in her quality is shown by the success of "The Ogilvies," which not only was popular with novel readers, but raised hopes that the writer possessed great dramatic power, to be more ably used when experience had corrected the crude faults of a first book. The story, based on passionate first love, is written with the enthusiasm and vigour which comes pleasantly from a

DINAH MULOCK (MRS. CRAIK)

young hand, and makes us disposed to view leniently the superabundance of sentiment which, under other circumstances, we should censure. The death of the boy, Leigh Pennythorne, is rendered with a pathos which calls for admiration, and we are not surprised to see it ranked with the death of little Paul Dombey; while that of Katherine Lynedon, spoken of at the time as possessing great dramatic force, strikes us now as melodramatic and sensational.

Encouraged by having found favour with the public, Miss Mulock followed up her success with "Olive" (1850), "Agatha's Husband" (1852), "Head of the Family" (1854). Her literary reputation was now established; and, though her *magnum opus*, "John Halifax," had yet to be written, it may be as well to consider some of the merits and weaknesses of her style, her treatment of her subjects, and her delineation of character.

In a short sketch, such as this, it is not possible to give a synopsis of the plots of the various books, or even, in most cases, extracts from them. We have to confine ourselves to the endeavour to realise the effect they produced at the time they were written—the estimation they were then held in, and to see what position they now command among the novels of the present day.

By MRS. PARR

Perhaps it will be only fair towards the faults we are about to find that we should recall the forward strides made by women in the past forty years. We who can recall the faulty teaching and the many prejudices of that date must often question if women now are sufficiently sensible of the advantages they possess.

A reviewer of Miss Mulock's novels, writing in 1866, says: "It is one of the chief misfortunes of almost every female novelist that her own education, as a woman, has been wretchedly defective;" and further on he adds: "the *education* of the majority of women leaves them not only without information, but without intelligent interest in any subject that does not immediately concern them." He then points out that it seems impossible for women to describe a man as he is—that they see him only from the outside. "They are ignorant of the machinery which sets the thing going, and the principle of the machinery; and so they discreetly tell you what kind of case it has, but nothing more."

Now, when the time has come that young men and maidens have other interests in common than those which spring out of flirtation and love-making, we may feel quite sure that each sex will get a better insight and have a juster knowledge of the other. The general taste for exercise, and the development of activity and health of

DINAH MULOCK (MRS. CRAIK)

body, has killed sentimentality and the heroines of the Rosa Matilda school. Not that these were the heroines that Miss Mulock created. Her ideals are to a certain extent made of flesh and blood, although they are not always living figures. Even at the period when we are told that "In the world of letters few authors have so distinct and at the same time so eminent a position as this lady," her judicious admirers find fault with her overflow of feminine sentimentality, which never permitted her ideal sufferers to conquer their griefs so far that they could take a practical and healthy interest in the affairs of the living world. "They live only 'for others'" says one critic, "'the beautiful light' is always in their faces; their hands 'work spasmodically' at least once in every two or three chapters."

Regarding the cramping influence of the prejudices which hedged in women in Miss Mulock's day, is it not very possible that this flaw in the portraiture of her own sex may have been due to the narrowness of her training rather than to any deficiency in her talent? Nothing more plainly shows how warped her judgment had become than many of the passages in "A Woman's Thoughts about Women." This is a book with much sound argument in it, and full of the desire to rectify the feminine grievances to which she was not blind. But when we come to a passage like the following, in which she asserts that all who "preach up lovely uselessness, fascinating frivolity, delicious helplessness, not only insult womanhood but her Creator," we ask how is this to be reconciled with the text which comes immediately after: "Equally blasphemous, and perhaps even more harmful, is the outcry about the equality of the sexes; the frantic attempt to force women, many of whom are either ignorant of, or unequal for, their own duties, into the position and duties of men. A pretty state of matters would ensue! Who that ever listened for two hours to the verbose confused inanities of a ladies' committee would immediately go and give his vote for a female House of Commons? or who, on receipt of a lady's letter of business—I speak of the average—would henceforth desire to have our courts of justice stocked with matronly lawyers and our colleges thronged by 'sweet girl graduates with their golden hair'? As for finance, if you pause to consider the extreme difficulty there always is in balancing Mrs. Smith's housekeeping book, or Miss Smith's quarterly allowance, I think, my dear Paternal Smith, you need not be much afraid lest this loud acclaim for women's rights should ever end in pushing you from your counting house, college, or elsewhere."

On this showing, such crass ignorance is to be accepted

DINAH MULOCK (MRS. CRAIK)

in women, and is to be taken as a matter of course and as natural to them as cutting their teeth or having measles or chicken pox. It is of little use to advocate "Self Dependence," "Female Professions," "Female Handicrafts," for those who cannot write a business letter or do a simple sum. Miss Mulock may have had, indeed I fear had, much reason to cast these reproaches at her sex. But that she did not feel their shame, and urge her sister women to strive for an education more worthy of intelligent beings, proves to me how deeply her mental gifts suffered from the cramping influence of the time in which she lived. Could she have enjoyed some of the advantages which spring out of the greater freedom of thought and action permitted in the present day, how greatly it would have enlarged her mental vision! Her male creations would have been cast in a more vigorous man-like mould. Her feminine ideals would no longer be incarnations of sentiment but living vital creatures. Where the mind is stunted the mental insight must be limited; and strong as were Miss Mulock's talents, they were never able to burst the bonds which for generations had kept the greater number of women in intellectual imprisonment.

In "Olive," the novel which immediately followed "The Ogilvies," Miss Mulock ventured on a very fresh and interesting subject. Olive, the heroine of the story, is a deformed girl, "a puir bit crippled lassie" with a crooked spine. To make this centre-character attractive and all-absorbing was a worthy effort on the part of an author, and we take up the book and settle ourselves to see how it will be done. Unfortunately, before long, the courage which conceived the personal blemish gives way, and, succumbing to the difficulties of making mind triumph over beauty, Miss Mulock commits the artistic error of trying to impress upon you that, notwithstanding the pages of lamentations over this deformity and the attack made on your sympathy, the disfigurement was so slight that no person could possibly have noticed it. Naturally this puts the heroine in a more commonplace position; and as several minor plots are introduced which Olive only serves to string together, much of the interest in her with which we started is frittered away.

Finally, Olive marries and restores the faith of a religious sceptic. And here it is curious to read the objections raised at the time against bringing into fiction "subjects most vital to the human soul." One critic, after describing the hero he is willing to accept—and, much to our regret, space prevents us showing this terrible model that we have escaped—says: "But a hero whose intellectual crotchets, or delusions, or blindness, are to be entrusted for repairs

DINAH MULOCK (MRS. CRAIK)

to a fascinating heroine—a mental perplexity which is to be solved in fiction—a deep-rooted scepticism which is to lose its *vis vitæ* according to the artistic demands of a tale of the fancy, this we cannot away with. Sceptics are not plastic and obliging. Would to Heaven scepticism *could* be cured by bright eyes, dulcet tones, and a novelist's art of love!"

Criticisms in this tone make more plain to us the difficulties which novelists in the fifties had to grapple with. So many subjects were tabooed, so many natural impulses restrained, while the bogey Propriety was flaunted to scare the most innocent actions, so that nothing short of genius could ride safely over such narrow-minded bigotry. That an extreme licence should follow before the happy mean could be arrived at, was a safe prediction; but many of the writers in that day must have had a hard task while trying to clip the wings of their soaring imaginations, so that they might not rise above the level marked out by Mrs. Grundy.

Now, all these social dogmas must have had an immense influence on the receptive mind of Dinah Mulock, and readers must not lose sight of this fact should they be inclined to call some of her books didactic, formal, or old-fashioned. She never posed as a brilliant, impassioned writer of stories which tell of wrongs, or crimes, or great mental conflicts. In her novels there is no dissection of character, no probing into the moral struggles of the human creature. Her teaching holds high the standard of duty, patience, and the unquestioning belief that all that God wills is well.

The enormous hold which, ever since its first appearance in 1857, "John Halifax" has had on a great portion of the English-speaking public, is due to the lofty elevation of its tone, its unsullied purity and goodness, combined with a great freshness, which appeals to the young and seems to put them and the book in touch with each other. Those who read the story years ago still recollect the charm it had for them; and, in a degree, the same fascination exists for youthful readers at the present time. The theme is noble, setting forth the high moral truth of "the nobility of man as man," and into its development the author threw all her powers.

From the opening sentence, where you are at once introduced to the ragged, muddy boy and the sickly helpless lad, you feel that these two will prove to be the leading actors in the story—probably made contrasts of, and perhaps played one against the other. This idea, however, is speedily dispelled. Possibly from a dread of failing where it is thought so many women do fail—in the

DINAH MULOCK (MRS. CRAIK)

portrayal of the unseen sides of character and the infinite subtleties it gives rise to—Miss Mulock, wisely we think, decided to place her story in the autobiographic form; and the gentle refined invalid, Phineas Fletcher, is made the *deus ex machina* to unravel to the reader not only the romance of his friend John Halifax's history, but also the working of his noble chivalrous nature. Few situations are more pathetically drawn than the attitude of these two lads, with its exchange of dependence and hero-worship on the one side, and of tender, helpful compassion on the other. A true David and Jonathan we see them, full of the trust, confidence, and sincerity young unsullied natures are capable of. And the story of the friendship, as it grows towards maturity, is equally well told.

His energy and his indomitable faith in himself make a prosperous man of the penniless boy. We follow him on from driving the skin cart to being master of the tanyard; and throughout all his temptations, struggles, success, he maintains the same honest, fearless spirit.

It seems natural that when to such an exalted nature love comes it should come encircled with romance, and the wooing of Ursula March, as told by sensitive, affectionate Phineas Fletcher, is very prettily described.

For the reason that Ursula is an heiress with a host of aristocratic relations, John believes his love for her to be hopeless. He struggles against this overwhelming passion for some time, until the continuous strain throws him into a fever of which his friend fears he will die. In this agonising strait Phineas is inspired with the idea of confessing the truth to Ursula; and, after a touching scene in which this is most delicately done, she determines to go to the man who is dying of love for her. In the interview, which is too long to be given in its entirety and too good to be curtailed, John tells her that owing to a great sorrow that has come to him he must leave Norton Bury and go to America. She begs to be told the reason, and without an actual avowal he lets her see his secret.

"'John, stay!'

"It was but a low, faint cry, like that of a little bird. But he heard it—felt it. In the silence of the dark she crept up to him, like a young bird to its mate, and he took her into the shelter of his love for evermore. At once all was made clear between them, for whatever the world might say they were in the sight of heaven equal, and she received as much as she gave."

When lights are brought into the room John takes Ursula's hand and leads her to where old Abel Fletcher is sitting.

"His head was erect, his eyes shining, his whole aspect that of a man who declares before all the world, 'This is

DINAH MULOCK (MRS. CRAIK)

my *own*.' 'Eh?' said my father, gazing at them from over his spectacles.

"John spoke brokenly, 'We have no parents, neither she nor I. Bless her—for she has promised to be my wife.'

"And the old man blessed her with tears."

Abel Fletcher, grave, stern, uncompromising—as members of the Society of Friends in that day were wont to be—is a clever study. He will not yield readily to the influence of John, and when he does give way it is by slow degrees. Yet one of the most winning traits in this somewhat over-perfect young man, given at times to impress his moral obligations rather brusquely, is the deference he pays to his former master and the filial affection he keeps for him; and the author manages in these scenes to put the two into excellent touch with each other—so that, through John's attitude to him, the hard close-fisted old tanner is transfigured into a patriarch who fitly gives his blessing to the bride, and later on, in a scene of great pathos, bestows his last benediction on her blind baby daughter.

It was said at the time of its publication, and it is still said, that in " John Halifax " Miss Mulock reached the summit of her power. That she felt this herself seems to be shown by her adopting the title of " Author of 'John Halifax.'" Its publication was in many ways a new departure. It was the first of that numerous series of books brought out by her (after) life-long friend, Mr. Blackett. Those were not the days when "twenty thousand copies were exhausted before a word of this novel was written;" yet the book had a remarkable and legitimate success. Of its merits a notable critic said, "If we could erase half a dozen sentences from this book it would stand as one of the most beautiful stories in the English language, conveying one of the highest moral truths." And that these few sentences, while in no way affecting the actual beauty of the story, are a blot and an "artistic and intellectual blunder—" the more to be deplored in a book whose moral teaching throughout is so excellent—we must confess. "The ragged boy, with his open, honest face, as he asks the respectable Quaker for work, is no beggar; the lad who drives the cart of dangling skins is not inferior to Phineas Fletcher, who watches for him from his father's windows and longs for his companionship; and the tanner—the honest and good man who marries Ursula March, a lady born—is her equal. Having shown that men in the sight of God are equal and that therefore all good men must be equal upon earth, what need that John should have in his keeping a little Greek Testament which he views as a most precious possession because in it is written 'Guy Halifax, Gentleman'? Are we to conclude that all his moral excellence and intellectual worth were derived from *ladies* and *gentlemen* who had been his remote ancestors, but with whom he had never been in personal contact at all, since at twelve years old he was a ragged orphan, unable to read and write?"

Miss Mulock could not have meant this, and yet she lays herself open to the charge, a kind of echo of which is heard in the adding to her good plain title of "John Halifax" the unnecessary tag, "Gentleman."

Her literary career being now fully established, Miss Mulock decided on taking up her permanent residence in London; and, about this time, she went to live at Wildwood, a cottage at North End, Hampstead. The now ubiquitous interviewer—that benefactor of those who want to know—had not then been called into being, so there is no record at hand to tell how the rooms were furnished, what the mistress wore, her likes, dislikes, and the various idiosyncrasies she displayed in half an hour's conversation. Such being the case we must be content with the simple fact that, charming by the candid sincerity of her disposition, and the many personal attractions that when young she possessed, Miss Mulock speedily drew around her a circle of friends whom, with rare fidelity, she ever after kept.

"John Halifax" was followed in 1859 by "A Life for a Life," a novel which, although it never obtained the same popularity, fully maintains the position won by its precursor. In it Miss Mulock breaks new ground both as to plot and the manner in which she relates the story, which is told by the hero and heroine in the form of a journal kept by each, so that we have alternate chapters of *his* story and *her* story. This form of construction is peculiar and occasionally presents to the reader some difficulties, but as a medium to convey opinions and convictions which the author desires to demonstrate it is happily conceived. The motive of the book is tragedy, the keynote murder—that is murder according to the exigencies of the story-teller. Max Urquhart, the hero—who at the time the tale opens is a staid, serious man of forty—is the perpetrator of this crime, committed at the age of nineteen in a fit of intoxication on a man named Johnston. Journeying from London to join a brother who is dying of consumption at Pau, Urquhart, through a mistake, finds that instead of being at Southampton he is at Salisbury. On the way he has made the acquaintance of the pseudo-driver of the coach, a flashy, dis-

DINAH MULOCK (MRS. CRAIK)

sipated fellow, who by a tissue of lies induces the raw Scotch lad to remain for some hours at the inn and then be driven on by him to where they will overtake the right coach. By this man young Urquhart is made drunk, and when as a butt he no longer amuses the sottish company they brutally turn him into the street. Later on he is aroused by the cut of a whip. It is his coach companion who pacifies him with the assurance that if he gets into the gig he will be speedily taken by him to Southampton. The lad consents, he is helped up and soon falls fast asleep to be awakened in the middle of Salisbury plain by his savage tormentor, who pushes him out and tells him to take up his lodging at Stonehenge. The poor youth, with just sufficient sense left in him to feel that he is being kept from his dying brother, implores the ruffian to take him on his way. "To the devil with your brother," is the answer, and in spite of all entreaties, Johnston whips up his horse, and is on the point of starting, when Urquhart, maddened by rage, catches him unawares, drags him from the gig, and, flings him violently on the ground, where his head strikes against one of the great stones, and he is killed.

How Urquhart manages to reach Southampton, and to get to Pau, he never knows; but when he does arrive at his destination, it is to find his brother dead and buried, and the fit of mania which follows is set down to the shock this gives him. At the end of a year, hearing that Johnston's death is attributed to accident, and being under the conviction that if the truth were told he would be hanged, he resolves to lock the secret in his own breast until the hour of his death draws near, and, in the meanwhile, to expiate his offence by living for others, and for the good he can do to them. He becomes an army doctor, goes through the Crimean War, and, when we are introduced to him, is doing duty at Aldershot, near where, at a ball, he meets the inevitable she, Theodora Johnston. If the hero is drawn dark, thin, with a spare, wiry figure, and a formal, serious air, the portrait of the heroine, with her undeniably ordinary figure, and a face neither pretty nor young, forms a fitting pendant to it. These two are irresistibly drawn towards each other, and, notwithstanding that the lady bears the fatal name of Johnston, they soon become engaged. Dr. Urquhart's tender conscience then demands that the tragic misdeed of his life shall be confessed to the woman he is about to make his wife, and, in a letter, he confides to her the sad history, adding, as postscript, some few days later: "I have found his grave at last." Here follows the inscription, which proves the dead man to have been the son of Theodora's father,

DINAH MULOCK (MRS. CRAIK)

her own half-brother, Henry Johnston. "Farewell, Theodora!"

It is impossible here to give more than this crude outline of the plot of a book in which, far beyond the story she means to tell, the author has her own individual opinions and convictions to impress on us. The temptation to earnest writers to try, through their writings, to make converts of their readers, is often very strong, and in this instance Miss Mulock undoubtedly gave way to it. She had not only a vehement abhorrence of capital punishment, but, to quote from her book, she maintained "that any sin, however great, being repented of and forsaken, is, by God, and ought to be by man, altogether pardoned, blotted out, and done away."

As was at the time said, "Her argument demands a stronger case than she has dared to put;" but so ably are the incidents strung together, so touchingly are the relative positions of these suffering souls described, that their sorrows, affection, and fidelity become convincing; and, full of the pathetic tragedy of the situation, we are oblivious of the fact that what is called a crime is nothing greater than an accident, a misfortune, and that for murder we must substitute manslaughter.

From the date of the appearance of "John Halifax,"

By MRS. PARR

Miss Mulock's pen was never long idle. Composition was not a labour to her; and friends who knew her at that time, describe her as walking about the room, or bending over on a low stool, rapidly setting down her thoughts in that small delicate writing which gave no trouble to read. She had beautiful hands; a tall, slim, graceful figure; and, with the exception of her mouth, which was too small, and not well shaped, delicate and regular features. These attractions, heightened by a charming frankness of manner, made her very popular. Her poetic vein was strong. She published several volumes of poems, and many of her verses, when set to music, became much admired as songs.

Following "A Life for a Life," came, in somewhat quick succession, "Studies from Life," "Mistress and Maid," "Christian's Mistake," "A Noble Life," "Two Marriages." These in a period of ten years.

As may be supposed, they are not all of equal merit; neither does any one of them touch the higher level of the author's earlier books. Still, there is good honest work in each, and the same exalted purity of tone, while much of the sentimentality complained of before is wholly omitted or greatly toned down.

"Mistress and Maid" is one of those good, quiet stories, full of homely truths and pleasant teaching, in

DINAH MULOCK (MRS. CRAIK)

which is shown the writer's quick sympathy with the working class. The maid, Elizabeth, is as full of character and of refined feelings as is Hilary Leaf, the mistress, and her one romance of love, although not so fortunate, has quite as much interest. The opening scenes, in which these two first meet, are excellent, giving us, all through their early association, touches of humour—a quality which, in Miss Mulock's writings, is very rare.

The picture of the rather tall, awkward, strongly built girl of fifteen, hanging behind her anxious-eyed, sad-voiced mother, who pushes her into notice with " I've brought my daughter, ma'am, as you sent word you'd take on trial. 'Tis her first place, and her'll be awk'ard like at first. Hold up your head, Elizabeth," is drawn with that graphic fidelity which gives interest to the most commonplace things in life. The awkward girl proves to be a rough diamond, capable of much polish, and by the kindly teaching of Hilary Leaf she is turned into an admirable, praiseworthy woman. One has to resist the temptation to say more about Hilary Leaf, an energetic, intelligent girl who, when she cannot make a living for herself and her sister by school-keeping, tries, and succeeds, by shop-keeping. The description of the struggles of these two poor ladies to pay their way, and keep up a respectable appearance, comes sympathetically from the pen of a woman whose heart was ever open to similar distresses in real life. To her praise be it remembered that to any tale of true suffering Dinah Mulock never closed her ears or her hand.

Her next two novels, "Christian's Mistake" and "A Noble Life," in our opinion, fall far short of any of her previous efforts. Yet they were both received with much popular favour, particularly the former, which called forth warm praise from reviewers.

For us not one of the characters has a spark of vitality. Christian is not even the shadow of a young girl made of flesh and blood. Her forbearance and self-abnegation are maddening. Her husband, the "Master of St. Bede's," twenty-five years her senior and a widower, is nothing but a lay figure, meant to represent a good man, but utterly devoid of intellect and, one would think, of feeling, since he permits his young bride, possessed of all the seraphic virtues, to be snubbed and brow-beaten by two vulgar shrewish sisters-in-law. There is no interest of plot or depicting of character, and the children are as unreal and offensive as their grown up relations. In "A Noble Life," also, there is nothing which stirs our sympathies. Even the personal deformities of the unfortunate little earl fail to touch us, and, when grown up and invested with every meritorious attribute, he is more like the "example" of a moral tale than a being of human nature.

As has been said, the portrayal of men is not this author's strong point. "Her sympathy with a good man is complete on the moral, but defective on the intellectual side"—a serious deficiency in one who has to create beings in whom we are asked to take a sustained interest.

That she could rise superior to this defect is shown in "The Woman's Kingdom." In this story Miss Mulock displays all her old charm of simplicity and directness, and is strong in her treatment of domestic life. At the outset she announces that it will be a thorough love story, and takes as her text that "love is the very heart of life, the pivot upon which its whole machinery turns, without which no human existence can be complete, and with which, however broken and worn in part, it can still go on working somehow, and working to a comparatively useful and cheerful end." This question we shall not stop to argue, but proceed with—we cannot say the plot, for of plot there is none; it is just an every-day version of the old, old story, given with admirable force and sweetness. It is said to appeal principally to young women, and it is possible that this is true, as the writer can recall the intense pleasure reading it gave to her nearly thirty years ago.

The book opens with the description of some seaside lodgings, in which we find twin sisters as opposite in character as in appearance. Edna is an epitome of all the virtues in a very plain binding. Letty, vain, spoilt, but loving her sister dearly, is a beauty. "Such women Nature makes rarely, very rarely; queens of beauty who instinctively take their places in the tournament of life, and rain influence upon weak mortals, especially men mortals." Two of the latter kind arrive as lodgers at the same house, brothers, also most dissimilar—Julius Stedman, impulsive, erratic and undisciplined; William, his elder brother, a grave, hard-working doctor, just starting practice. The four speedily become acquaintances —friends—and when they part are secretly lovers. Letty, by reason of what she calls "her unfortunate appearance," never doubts but that she has conquered both brothers; but happily it is to Edna that the young doctor has given his heart; and when in time Letty hears the news, "and remembers that she had been placing herself and Dr. Stedman in the position of the Irish ballad couplet,

>   Did ye ever hear of Captain Baxter,
>   Whom Miss Biddy refused afore he axed her?

her vanity was too innocent and her nature too easy to bear offence long."

DINAH MULOCK (MRS. CRAIK)

"But to think that after all the offers I have had you should be the first to get married, or anyhow, engaged! Who would ever have expected such a thing?" "Who would, indeed?" said Edna, in all simplicity, and with a sense almost of contrition for the fact. "Well, never mind," answered Letty consolingly, "I am sure I hope you will be very happy; and as for me"—she paused and sighed—"I should not wonder if I were left an old maid after all, in spite of my appearance."

But to be left an old maid is not to be Letty's fate. Julius, already bewitched by her beauty through being much more thrown into her society, falls passionately in love with her, and for lack of any one else, and because his ardour flatters and amuses her, Letty encourages him, permits an engagement, and promises to join him in India. But on the voyage out she meets a rich Mr. Vanderdecken, with whom she lands at the Cape, and whom she marries. This is the tragic note in the happy story, the one drop of gall in the Stedmans' cup of felicity. Edna and her husband are patterns of domestic well-being. The joys and cares of every-day life have mellowed all that was good in them, and the account given of their home and their family is one we dwell upon lovingly.

Perhaps it is but natural that in our later reading we should note some small discrepancies that had formerly escaped us. We regret that the sisters had drifted so widely apart, and that each should seem to be so unconcerned at the distance which divides them. It is as if happiness can make us callous as well as luxury. And although it was true that Letty's desertion suddenly wrecked the hopes of her lover, it seems hardly probable that such an unstable being as Julius would have taken her falseness so seriously. A wiser man might have foreseen the possibility.

Still, when this and more is said, our liking for the story remains as strong as ever. We know of few books which give a better picture of healthful domestic happiness and pure family life.

Although we have hitherto called, and shall continue to call, our authoress by her maiden name, she had in 1864 changed it by marrying Mr. G. Lillie Craik, a partner in the house of Macmillan & Co., and shortly after she removed to Shortlands, near Bromley, in Kent. This change in her state does not appear to have interfered with her occupation, and for many years volume followed volume in quick succession.

Unwisely, we think, for her literary reputation, she was led, through her strong sympathy, to advocate marriage with a deceased wife's sister in a novel, published in 1871, called "Hannah."

DINAH MULOCK (MRS. CRAIK)

The novel with a purpose is almost certain to fall into the error of giving the argument on one side only. Its author has rarely any toleration for the ethical aspect of the other side of the question, and it is to be doubted if such books ever advance the cause they desire to advocate. In "Hannah" we are perfectly surfeited by those who wish to marry within the forbidden degree, and we feel as little toleration for the placid Bernard Rivers—one of those men who never believe in the pinch of a shoe until they want to put it on their own feet—as for Jim Dixon, who, after evading the law, speedily grows tired of the deceased wife's sister, and avails himself of his legal advantage to take another wife.

The objections we feel to novels of this class are well stated by a writer in the *Edinburgh Review*, No. clxxxix. "We object," he says, "on principle to stories written with the purpose of illustrating an opinion, or establishing a doctrine. We consider this an illegitimate use of fiction. Fiction may be rightfully employed to impress upon the public mind an acknowledged truth, or to revive a forgotten woe—never to prove a disputed one. Its appropriate aims are the delineation of life, the exhibition and analysis of character, the portraiture of passion, the description of nature."

In most of these aims Miss Mulock had proved herself

an expert. In addition to her numerous novels and volumes of poems, she wrote a large number of tales for children, many of which, I am told, are exceedingly charming. One cannot read her books without being struck by the intense affection she felt for children. She had none of her own, but she adopted a daughter to whom she gave a mother's love and care. From time to time there appeared from her pen volumes of short stories, studies, and essays; but it is not by these that her name and fame will be kept green. Neither will her reputation rest on her later novels. This she must have realised herself when writing, "Brains, even if the strongest, will only last a certain time and do a certain quantity of work—really good work." Miss Mulock had begun to work the rich vein of her imagination at an early age. She took few holidays, and gave herself but little rest.

She was by no means what is termed a literary woman. She was not a great reader; and although much praise is due to the efforts she made to improve herself, judged by the present standard, her education remained very defective. That she lacked the fire of genius is true, but it is no less true that she was gifted with great imaginative ability and the power of depicting ordinary men and women leading upright, often noble lives.

The vast public that such books as hers appeal to is

DINAH MULOCK (MRS. CRAIK)

shown in the large circulation of some of her works, the sale of "John Halifax, Gentleman" amounting to 250,000 copies, 80,000 of which—the sixpenny edition—have been sold within the last few months. This shows that her popularity is not confined to any one class. The gospel she wrote was for all humanity.

As a woman, she was loved best by those who knew her best. "Dinah was far more clever than her books," said an old friend who had been recalling pleasant memories to repeat to me. She died suddenly on the 12th of October 1887, from failure of the heart's action—the death she had described in the cases of Catherine Ogilvie, of John Halifax, and of Ursula, his wife—the death she had always foreseen for herself.

Around her grave in Keston churchyard stood a crowd of mourners—rich, poor, old and young—sorrowing for the good loyal friend who had gone from them, whose face they should see no more.

Louisa Parr

JULIA KAVANAGH, AMELIA BLANDFORD EDWARDS

By MRS. MACQUOID

JULIA KAVANAGH. AMELIA BLANDFORD EDWARDS

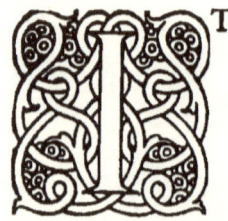IT is difficult to think of two writers more strongly contrasted, judging from the revelation their books afford of their natures and ways of thought. They both strove, in their novels, to represent individual specimens of humanity. They must both have possessed the power of distinct vision; but though Miss Kavanagh was a keen observer of externals, her types seem to have been created by imaginative faculty rather than by insight into real men and women, while Miss Edwards appears to have gone about the world open-eyed, and with note-book in hand, so vivid are some of her portraits.

In traditions, also, these writers differ. Miss Kavanagh has complete faith in the old French motto, "le bon sang

JULIA KAVANAGH

ne peut pas mentir;" while one of Miss Edwards's heroes, an aristocrat by birth, is extremely happy as a merchant captain, with his plebeian Italian wife.

The two writers, however, strike the same note in regard to some of their female personages. Both Barbara Churchill and Nathalie Montolieu are truthful to rudeness.

JULIA KAVANAGH never obtrudes her personality on the reader, though she lifts him into the exquisitely pure and peaceful atmosphere which one fancies must have been hers. There is something so restful in her books, that it is difficult to believe she was born no longer ago than 1824, and that only twenty years ago she died in middle life; she seems to belong to a farther-away age—probably because her secluded life kept her strongly linked to the past, out of touch with the new generation and the new world of thought around her.

She began to write for magazines while still very young, and was only twenty-three when her first book, "The Three Paths," a child's story, was published. After this she wrote about fourteen novels, the best known of which are "Madeleine," "Nathalie," and "Adèle." She wrote many short stories, some of which were reprinted in volumes—notably the collection called "Forget-me-nots," published after her death. She also wrote "A Summer and Winter in the two Sicilies," "Woman in France in the 18th Century," "Women of Christianity," and two books which seem to have been highly praised—"Englishwomen of Letters" and "Frenchwomen of Letters."

Julia Kavanagh's first novel, "Madeleine," appeared in 1848—a charming story, its scene being in the Auvergne. The beginning is very striking, the theme being somewhat like that of "Bertha in the Lane"; but Madeleine, when she has given up her false lover, devotes the rest of her life to founding and caring for an orphanage.

Born in Ireland, Julia Kavanagh spent the days of her youth in Normandy, and the scene of her second novel, "Nathalie," is Norman, though Nathalie herself is a handsome, warm-blooded Provençale. The scenery and surroundings are very life-like, but, with one exception, the people are less attractive than they are in "Adèle." In both books one feels a wish to eliminate much of the interminable talk, which could easily be dispensed with.

Nathalie, the country doctor's orphan daughter, teacher to the excellently drawn schoolmistress, Mademoiselle Dantin, is sometimes disturbingly rude and tactless, in spite of her graceful beauty. With all this *gaucherie*, and a violent temper to boot, Nathalie exercises a singular fascination over the people of the story, especially over the delightful Canoness, Aunt Radégonde, who is to me the most real of Miss Kavanagh's characters. Madame Radégonde de Sainville is a true old French lady of fifty years ago, as charming as she is natural.

The men in Julia Kavanagh's books have led secluded lives, or they are extremely reserved—very hard nuts indeed to crack for the ingenuous, inexperienced girls on whom they bestow their lordly affection. One does not pity Nathalie, who certainly brings her troubles on herself; but in the subsequent book, sweet little Adèle is too bright a bit of sunshine to be sacrificed to such a being as William Osborne.

The old château in which Adèle has spent her short life is in the north-east of France; its luxuriant but neglected garden, full of lovely light and shade, its limpid lake, and the old French servants, are delightfully fresh. The chapters which describe these are exquisite reading—

a gentle idyll glowing with sunshine, and with a leisureful charm that makes one resent the highly coloured intrusion of the Osborne family, though the Osborne women afford an effective contrast. Adèle is scantily educated, but she is always delightful, though we are never allowed to forget that she is descended from the ancient family of de Courcelles. She is thoroughly amiable and much enduring, in spite of an occasional waywardness.

Fresh and full of beauty as these novels are, with their sweet pure-heartedness, their truth and restful peace, they cannot compare with the admirable short sketches of the quiet side of French life by the same writer. The scenes in which the characters of these short stories are set, show the truth of Julia Kavanagh's observation, as well as the quality of her style; they are quite as beautiful as some of Guy de Maupassant's little gem-like Norman stories, but they are perfectly free from cynicism, although she truly shows the greedy grasping nature of the Norman peasant. The gifts of this writer are intensified, and more incisively shown, in these sketches because they contain few superfluous words and conversations. Julia Kavanagh must have revelled in the creation of such tales as "By the Well," and its companions; they are steeped in joyous brightness, toned here and there with real pathos as in "Clément's Love" and "Annette's Love-Story," in the collection called "Forget-me-nots."

Such a story as "By the Well" would nowadays be considered a lovely idyll, and, by critics able to appreciate its breadth and finished detail, a Meissonier in point of execution: it glows with true colour.

Fifine Delpierre is not a decked-out peasant heroine; she is a bare-footed, squalid, half-clothed, half-starved little girl, when we first see her beside the well. This is the scene that introduces her.

"It has a roof, as most wells have in Normandy, a low thatched roof, shaggy, brown, and old, but made rich and gorgeous when the sun shines upon it by many a tuft of deep green fern, and many a cluster of pink sedum and golden stonecrop. Beneath that roof, in perpetual shade and freshness, lies the low round margin, built of heavy ill-jointed stones, grey and discoloured with damp and age; and within this spreads an irregular but lovely fringe of hart's-tongue. The long glossy leaves of a cool pale green grow in the clefts of the inner wall, so far as the eye can reach, stretching and vanishing into the darkness, at the bottom of which you see a little tremulous circle of watery light. This well is invaluable to the Lenuds, for, as they pass by the farm the waters of the little river grow brackish and unfit for use. So long ago, before they were rich, the Lenuds having discovered this spring through the means of a neighbouring mason, named Delpierre, got him to sink and make the well, in exchange for what is called a servitude in French legal phrase; that is to say, that he and his were to have the use of the well for ever and ever. Bitter strife was the result of this agreement. The feud lasted generations, during which the Lenuds throve and grew rich, and the Delpierres got so poor, that, at the time when this story opens, the last had just died leaving a widow and three children in bitter destitution. Maître Louis Lenud, for the Parisian Monsieur had not yet reached Manneville, immediately availed himself of this fact to bolt and bar the postern-door through which his enemy had daily invaded the courtyard to go to the well.

"'It was easily done, and it cost me nothing—not a sou,' exultingly thought Maître Louis Lenud, coming to this conclusion for the hundredth time on a warm evening in July. The evening was more than warm, it was sultry; yet Maître Louis sat by the kitchen fire watching his old servant, Madeleine, as she got onion soup ready for the evening meal, utterly careless of the scorching blaze which shot up the deep dark funnel of the chimney. Pierre, his son, unable to bear this additional heat, stood in the open doorway, waiting with the impatience of eighteen for his supper, occasionally looking out on the farmyard, grey and quiet at this hour, but oftener casting a glance within. The firelight danced about the stone kitchen, now lighting up the *armoire* in the corner, with cupids and guitars, and shepherds' pipes and tabors, and lovers' knots carved on its brown oak panels; now showing the lad the bright copper saucepans, hung in rows upon the walls; now revealing the stern grim figure of his father, with his heavy grey eyebrows and his long Norman features both harsh and acute; and very stern could Maître Louis look, though he wore a faded blue blouse, an old handkerchief round his neck, and on his head a white cotton nightcap, with a stiff tassel to it; now suddenly subsiding and leaving all in the dim uncertain shadows of twilight.

During one of these grey intervals, the long-drawling Norman voice of Maître Louis spoke:

"'The Delpierres have given up the well,' he said, with grim triumph.

"'Ay, but Fifine comes and draws water every night,' tauntingly answered Pierre.

"'Hem!' the old man exclaimed with a growl.

"'Fifine comes and draws water every night,' reiterated Pierre."

He had seen the eldest child Fifine, a girl of eight or ten, sitting on her doorstep singing her little brother to sleep, with a wreath of hart's-tongue round her head, and a band of it round her waist. "And a little beggar, too, she looked," scornfully added Pierre, "with her uncombed hair and her rags."

"'Shall we let the dog loose to-night?' he said."

Maître Louis uttered his deepest growl, and promised to break every bone in his son's body if he attempted such a thing.

"Pierre silently gulped down his onion soup, but the 'do it if you dare' of the paternal wink only spurred him on. He gave up the dog as too cruel, but not his revenge.

"The night was a lovely one and its tender subdued meaning might have reached Pierre's heart, but did not. He saw as he crouched in the grass near the old well that the full round moon hung in the sky; he saw that the willows by the little river looked very calm and still" . . . [the revengeful lad watches for the child and falls asleep, then wakes suddenly].

"Behold there was little Fifine with her pitcher standing in the moonlight. She stood there with her hair falling about her face, her torn bodice, her scanty petticoats, and her little bare feet. How the little traitress had got in, whilst he, the careless dragon, slept, Pierre could not imagine; but she was evidently quite unconscious of his presence. . . . The child set her pitcher down very softly, shook back the hanging hair from her face, and peeped into the well. She liked to look thus into that deep dark hole, with its damp walls clothed with the long green hart's-tongue that had betrayed her. She liked also to look at that white circle of water below; for you see if there was a wrathful Adam by her, ready for revenge, she was a daughter of Eve, and Eve-like enjoyed the flavour of this forbidden fruit. . . . Fifine took up her pitcher again and walked straight on to the river. Pierre stared amazed, then suddenly he understood it all. There was an old forgotten gap in the hedge beyond the little stream, and through that gap Fifine and her pitcher nightly invaded Maître Louis Lenud's territory. . . . Having picked up a sharp flint which lay in the grass Pierre rose and bided his opportunity. Fifine went on till she had half-crossed a bridge-like plank which spanned the stream, then, as her ill-luck would have it, she stood still to listen to the distant hooting of an owl in the old church tower on the hill. Pierre saw the child's black figure in the moonlight standing out clearly against the background of grey willows, he saw the white plank and the dark river tipped with light flowing on beneath it. Above all, he saw Fifine's glazed pitcher, bright as silver; he was an unerring marksman, and he took a sure aim at this. The flint sped swiftly through the air; there was a crash, a low cry, and all was suddenly still. Both Fifine and her pitcher had tumbled into the river below and vanished there."

Pierre rescues her, and when Fifine has been for some years in service with the repentant Pierre's cousin her improved looks and clothing make her unrecognisable to the thick-headed well-meaning young farmer.

The only fault that can be found with these chronicles of Manneville is the likeness between them. The "Miller of Manneville," in the "Forget-me-not" collection, is full of charm, but it too much resembles "By the Well." The "Story of Monique" gives, however, a happy variety, and Monique is a thorough French girl; so is Mimi in the bright little story called "Mimi's Sin." Angélique again, in "Clément's Love," is a girl one meets with over and over again in Normandy, but these Norman stories are all so exquisitely told that it is invidious to single out favourites.

The stories laid in England, in which the characters are English, are less graphic; they lack the fresh and true atmosphere of their fellows placed across the Channel.

AMELIA BLANDFORD EDWARDS

Julia Kavanagh died at Nice, where she spent the last few years of her life. Had she lived longer she would perhaps have given us some graphic stories from the Riviera, for it is evident that foreign people and foreign ways attracted her sympathies so powerfully that she was able to reproduce them in their own atmosphere. In a brief but touching preface to the collection called "Forget-me-nots," published after her death, Mr. C. W. Wood gives us a lovable glimpse of this charming writer; reading this interesting little sketch deepens regret that one had not the privilege of personally knowing so sweet a woman.

IN regard to truth of atmosphere in her foreign stories, Julia Kavanagh certainly surpasses Amelia B. Edwards. In "Barbara's History," in "Lord Brackenbury," and in other stories by Miss Edwards, there are beautiful and graphic descriptions of foreign scenery, and we meet plenty of foreign people; but we feel that the latter are described by an Englishwoman who has taken an immense amount of pains to make herself acquainted with their ways and their speech—they somewhat lack spontaneity. In the two novels named there are chapters so full of local history and association that one thinks it might be well to have the books for companions when visiting the places described ; they are full of talent—in some places near akin to genius.

"Barbara's History" contains a great deal of genuine humour. It is a most interesting and exciting story, though in parts stagey ; the opening chapters, indeed the whole of Barbara's stay at her great-aunt's farm of Stoneycroft, are so excellent that one cannot wonder the book was a great success. Now and again passages and characters remind one of Dickens ; the great-aunt, Mrs. Sandyshaft, is a thorough Dickens woman, with a touch of the great master's exaggeration ; Barbara's father is another Dickens character. There are power and passion as well as humour in this book, but in spite of its interest it becomes fatiguing when Barbara leaves her aunt and the hundred pigs.

There is remarkable truth of characterisation in some of this writer's novels. Hugh Farquhar is sometimes an eccentric bore, but he is real. Barbara Churchill at times is wearyingly pedantic ; then, again, she is just as delightfully original—her first meeting with Mrs. Sandyshaft is so inimitable that I must transcribe a part of it.

A rich old aunt has invited Barbara Churchill, a

neglected child of ten years old, to stay with her in Suffolk. Barbara is the youngest of Mr. Churchill's three girls, and she is not loved by either her widowed father or her sisters, though an old servant named Goody dotes on the child. Barbara is sent by stage-coach from London to Ipswich :—

"Dashing on between the straggling cottages, and up a hill so closely shaded by thick trees that the dusk seems to thicken suddenly to-night, we draw up all at once before a great open gate, leading to a house of which I can only see the gabled outline and the lighted windows.

"The guard jumps down; the door is thrown open; and two persons, a man and a woman, come hurrying down the path.

"'One little girl and one box, as per book,' says the guard, lifting me out and setting me down in the road, as if I were but another box, to be delivered as directed.

"'From London?' asks the woman sharply.

"'From London,' replies the guard, already scrambling back to his seat; 'All right, ain't it?'

"'All right.'

"Whereupon the coach plunges on again into the dusk; the man shoulders my box as though it were a feather; and the woman who looks strangely gaunt and grey by this uncertain light, seizes me by the wrist and strides away towards the house at a pace that my cramped and weary limbs can scarcely accomplish.

"Sick and bewildered, I am hurried into a cheerful room where the table is spread as if for tea and supper, and a delicious perfume of coffee and fresh flowers fills the air; and—and, all at once even in the moment when I am first observing them, these sights and scents grow all confused and sink away together, and I remember nothing . . . . when I recover, I find myself laid upon a sofa, with my cloak and bonnet off, my eyes and mouth full of Eau de Cologne, and my hands smarting under a volley of slaps, administered by a ruddy young woman on one side, and by the same gaunt person who brought me in from the coach on the other. Seeing me look up, they both desist; and the latter, drawing back a step or two, as if to observe me to greater advantage, puts on an immense pair of heavy gold spectacles, stares steadily for some seconds, and and at length says:

"'What did you mean by that now?'

"Unprepared for so abrupt a question, I lie as if fascinated by her bright grey eyes, and cannot utter a syllable.

"'Are you better?'

"Still silent, I bow my head feebly, and keep looking at her.

"'Hey now. Am I a basilisk? Are you dumb, child?'

"Wondering why she speaks to me thus, and being, moreover, so very weak and tired, what can I do, but try in vain to answer, and failing in the effort, burst into tears again? Hereupon she frowns, pulls off her glasses, shakes her head angrily, and, saying: 'That's done to aggravate me, I know it is,' stalks away to the window, and stands there grimly, looking out upon the night. The younger woman, with a world of kindness in her rosy face . . . . whispers me not to cry.

"'That child's hungry,' says the other coming suddenly back. 'That's what's the matter with her. She's hungry, I know she is, and I won't be contradicted. Do you hear me, Jane?—I won't be contradicted.'

"'Indeed, ma'am, I think she is hungry, and tired too, poor little thing.'

"'Tired and hungry! . . . Mercy alive, then why don't she eat? Here's food enough for a dozen people. Child, what will you have? Ham, cold chicken pie, bread, butter, cheese, tea, coffee, ale?'

". . . . Everything tastes delicious; and not even the sight of the gaunt housekeeper . . . . has power to spoil my enjoyment.

"For she is the housekeeper, beyond a doubt. Those

heavy gold spectacles, that sad-coloured gown, that cap with its plain close bordering can belong to no one but a housekeeper. Wondering within myself that she should be so disagreeable; then where my aunt herself can be; why she has not yet come to welcome me; how she will receive me when she does come; and whether I shall have presence of mind enough to remember all the curtseys I have been drilled to make, and all the speeches I have been taught to say, I find myself eating as though nothing at all had been the matter with me, and even staring now and then quite confidently at my opposite neighbour.... Left alone now with the sleeping dogs and the housekeeper —who looks as if she never slept in her life—I find the evening wearisome. Observing too that she continues to look at me in the same grim imperturbable way, and seeing no books anywhere about, it occurs to me that a little conversation would perhaps be acceptable, and that, as I am her mistress's niece, it is my place to speak first.

"'If you please, ma'am,' I begin after a long hesitation.

"'HEY?'"

"Somewhat disconcerted by the sharpness and suddenness of this interruption, I pause, and take some moments to recover myself.

"'If you please, ma'am, when am I to see my aunt?'

"'Hey? What? Who?'

AMELIA BLANDFORD EDWARDS

"'My aunt, if you please, ma'am?'

"'Mercy alive! and pray who do you suppose I am?'

"'You, ma'am,' I falter, with a vague uneasiness impossible to describe; 'are you not the housekeeper?'

"To say that she glares vacantly at me from behind her spectacles, loses her very power of speech, and grows all at once quite stiff and rigid in her chair, is to convey but a faint picture of the amazement with which she receives this observation.

"'I,' she gasps at length, 'I! Gracious me, child, I am your aunt.' I feel my countenance become an utter blank. I am conscious of turning red and white, hot and cold, all in one moment. My ears tingle; my heart sinks within me; I can neither speak nor think. A dreadful silence follows, and in the midst of this silence my aunt, without any kind of warning, bursts into a grim laugh, and says:

"'Barbara, come and kiss me.'

"I could have kissed a kangaroo just then, in the intensity of my relief; and so getting up quite readily, touch her gaunt cheek with my childish lips, and look the gratitude I dare not speak. To my surprise she draws me closer to her knee, passes one hand idly through my hair, looks not unkindly, into my wondering eyes, and murmurs more to herself than me, the name of 'Barbara.'

"This gentle mood is, however, soon dismissed, and as if

ashamed of having indulged it, she pushes me away, frowns, shakes her head, and says quite angrily:

"'Nonsense, child, nonsense. It's time you went to bed.'"

[Next morning at breakfast.]

"'Your name,' said my aunt, with a little off-hand nod, 'is Bab. Remember that.'" . . . [Mrs. Sandyshaft asks her great niece why she took her for the housekeeper; the child hesitates, and at last owns that it was because of her dress.]

. . . . "'Too shabby?'

"'N—no, ma'am, not shabby; but . . . .'

"'But what? You must learn to speak out, Bab. I hate people who hesitate.'

"'But Papa said you were so rich, and . . . .'

"'Ah! He said I was rich did he? Rich! Oho! And what more, Bab? What more? Rich indeed! Come, you must tell me. What else did he say when he told you I was rich?'

"'N—nothing more, ma'am,' I replied, startled and confused by her sudden vehemence. 'Indeed nothing more.'

"'Bab!' said my aunt bringing her hand down so heavily upon the table that the cups and saucers rang again, 'Bab, that's false. If he told you I was rich, he told you how to get my money by-and-by. He told you to cringe and fawn, and worm yourself into my favour, to profit by my death, to be a liar, a flatterer, and a beggar, and why? Because I am rich. Oh yes, because I am rich.'

"I sat as if stricken into stone, but half comprehending what she meant, and unable to answer a syllable.

"'Rich indeed!' she went on, excited more and more by her own words and stalking to and fro between the window and the table, like one possessed. 'Aha! we shall see, we shall see. Listen to me, child. I shall leave you nothing —not a farthing. Never expect it—never hope for it. If you are good and true, and I like you, I shall be a friend to you while I live; but if you are mean and false, and tell me lies, I shall despise you. Do you hear? I shall despise you, send you home, never speak to you, or look at you again. Either way, you will get nothing by my death. Nothing—nothing!'

"My heart swelled within me—I shook from head to foot. I tried to speak and the words seemed to choke me.

"'I don't want it,' I cried passionately. 'I—I am not mean. I have told no lies—not one.'

"My aunt stopped short, and looked sternly down upon me, as if she would read my very soul.

"'Bab,' said she, 'do you mean to tell me that your father said nothing to you about why I may have asked you here, or what might come of it? Nothing? Not a word?'

"'He said it might be for my good—he told Miss Whymper to make me curtsey and walk better, and come into a room properly; he said he wished me to please you. That was all. He never spoke of money, or of dying, or of telling lies—never.'

"'Well then,' retorted my aunt, sharply, 'he meant it.'

"Flushed and trembling in my childish anger, I sprang from my chair and stood before her, face to face.

"'He did not mean it,' I cried. 'How dare you speak so of Papa? How dare . . . .'

"I could say no more, but, terrified at my own impetuosity, faltered, covered my face with both hands, and burst into an agony of sobs.

"'Bab,' said my aunt, in an altered voice, 'little Bab,' and took me all at once in her two arms, and kissed me on the forehead.

"My anger was gone in a moment. Something in her tone, in her kiss, in my own heart, called up a quick response; and nestling close in her embrace, I wept passionately. Then she sat down, drew me on her knee, smoothed my hair with her hand, and comforted me as if I had been a little baby.

"'So brave,' said she, 'so proud, so honest. Come, little Bab, you and I must be friends.'

"And we were friends from that minute; for from that minute a mutual confidence and love sprang up between us. Too deeply moved to answer her in words, I only clung the closer, and tried to still my sobs. She understood me.

"'Come,' said she, after a few seconds of silence, 'let's go and see the pigs.'"

The sketch of Hilda Churchill is very good, and so is that of the Grand Duke of Zollenstrasse. Taken as a whole, if we leave out the concluding chapters, "Barbara's History" is a stirring, original, and very amusing book, full of historical and topographical information, written in terse and excellent English, and very rich in colour—the people in it are so wonderfully alive.

"Lord Brackenbury" is very clever and full of pictures, but it lacks the brightness and the originality of "Barbara's History." Amelia B. Edwards wrote several other novels—"Half a Million of Money," "Miss Carew," "Debenham's Vow," &c. &c. She also published a

By MRS. MACQUOID

collection of short tales—"Monsieur Maurice," etc.—and a book of ballads. Born in 1831, she began to write at a time when sensational stories were in fashion, and produced a number of exciting stories—"The Four-fifteen Express," "The Tragedy in the Bardello Palace," "The Patagonian Brothers"—all extremely popular; though, when we read them now, they seem wanting in the insight into human nature so remarkably shown in some of her novels.

She was a distinguished Egyptologist, and the foundation in 1883 of the Egypt Exploration Fund was largely due to her efforts; she became one of the secretaries to this enterprise, and wrote a good deal on Egyptian subjects for European and American periodicals. She wrote and illustrated some interesting travel books, especially her delightful "A Thousand Miles up the Nile," and an account of her travels in 1872 among the—at that time—rarely visited Dolomites. The latter is called "Untrodden Peaks and Unfrequented Valleys:" it is interesting, but not so bright as the Nile book.

When one considers that a large part of her output involved constant and laborious research—that for the purposes of many of the books she had to take long and fatiguing journeys—the amount of good work she accomplished is very remarkable; the more so, because she was not only a writer, but an active promoter of some of the public movements of her time. She was a member of the Biblical Archæological Society—a member, too, of the Society for the Promotion of Hellenic Literature. Then she entered into the woman's question, not so popular in those days as it is in these, and was vice-president of a Society for promoting Women's Suffrage.

It is difficult to understand how in so busy and varied a life she could have found sufficient leisure for writing fiction; but she had a very large mental grasp, and probably as large a power of concentration. Remembering that she was an omnivorous reader, a careful student, possessed too of an excellent memory, we need not wonder at the fulness and richness of her books.

Katharine S. Macquoid

MRS. NORTON
By MRS. ALEXANDER

MRS. NORTON

IT is hardly necessary to state that this beautiful and charming woman was the second daughter of Thomas Sheridan and grand-daughter of Richard Brinsley Sheridan, of Regency renown. She was one of three sisters famous for beauty and brains, the eldest of whom married Lord Dufferin, and the youngest Lord Seymour, afterwards Duke of Somerset.

Born in the first decade of the present century, she married at nineteen, in 1827, George Norton, brother of the third Lord Grantley—a union which proved most unhappy. In 1836 Mr. Norton sought for a divorce, in an action which entirely failed. Nevertheless, Norton remained irreconcilable, and availed himself of all the powers which the law then lent to a vindictive husband, claiming the proceeds of his wife's literary work, and interfering between her and her children. But it is with

MRS. NORTON

Mrs. Norton as a writer rather than as a woman that we are concerned, and it is useless now to dwell upon the story of her wrongs and struggles.

Previous to this unfortunate suit she produced, in 1829, "The Story of Rosalie, with other Poems," which seems to have been her first published work. This was well received and much admired.

In 1830 "The Undying One," a poem on the Wandering Jew, was brought out, followed in 1840 by "The Dream and other Poems." This was highly praised in the *Quarterly Review* by Lockhart, who spoke of her as "the Byron of poetesses." Other poems from her pen touched on questions of social interest: "A Voice from the Factories" and "The Child of the Islands," a poem on the social condition of the English people. She also printed "English Laws for Women in the Nineteenth Century," and published much of it in pamphlets on Lord Cranworth's Divorce Bill of this year (1853), thus assisting in the amelioration of the laws relating to the custody of children, and the protection of married women's earnings.

Her natural tendency was towards poetry, and the first five books published by her were all in verse. In 1851 appeared a novel, in three volumes, called "Stuart of Dunleath," which was succeeded by "Lost and Saved" and "Old Sir Douglas."

By MRS. ALEXANDER

It is curious to observe the depth and width of the gulf which yawns between the novel of 1851 and the novel of to-day.

The latter opens with some brief sentence spoken by one of the characters, or a short dialogue between two or three of them, followed by a rapid sketch of their position or an equally brief picture of the scene in which the action of the piece is laid. The reader is plunged at once into the drama, and left to guess the parts allotted by the author to his puppets.

Forty-five years ago, when Mrs. Norton wrote "Stuart of Dunleath," the reader had to pass through a wide porch and many long passages before he reached the inner chambers of the story. An account of the hero and heroine's families, even to the third and fourth generation, was indispensable, and the minutest particulars of their respective abodes and surroundings were carefully detailed. The tale travelled by easy stages, with many a pause where byways brought additional wayfarers to join the throng of those already travelling through the pages; while each and all, regardless of proportion, were described with equal fulness whatever their degree of importance.

These are the characteristics of Mrs. Norton's novels, which stretch in a leisurely fashion to something like two hundred thousand words. Nevertheless, "Stuart of Dunleath" shows great ability and knowledge of the world. It is evidently written by a well-read, cultivated, and refined woman, with warm feelings and strong religious convictions. The descriptions are excellent, the language is easy and graceful.

The scene of the story lies chiefly in Scotland, and the Scotch characters are very well drawn, save one, Lady Macfarren, who is inhumanly hard. This, too, is one of the peculiarities of the forty or forty-five year old novel; its people are terribly consistent in good or evil. The dignity, the high-mindedness, the angelic purity of the heroine is insupportable, and the stainless honour, the stern resistance to temptation, the defiance of tyrannical wrongdoers, makes the hero quite as bad.

In "Stuart of Dunleath," however, the hero is decidedly weak. He is the guardian of Eleanor Raymond, the heroine, and, seeing a probability of making a large profit by a speculative loan, risks her money, hoping to obtain the means to buy back his estate without diminishing her fortune. The speculation fails. Eleanor is reduced to poverty, and Stuart is supposed to drown himself. Then the impoverished heroine, who is desperately in love with her guardian, is compelled to marry a wealthy baronet, Sir Stephen Penrhyn. This is the beginning of troubles, and very bad troubles they are, continuing steadily through two-thirds of the book.

Sir Stephen is a brutally bad husband, is shamelessly unfaithful, personally violent, breaks his wife's arm, and makes her life a burden. Her little twin sons are drowned in a boating accident, and then Stuart returns from the grave, having been stopped in his attempt to drown himself by a picturesque old clergyman, and started off to America, where he manages to recover the lost fortune.

By his advice, Eleanor leaves her tyrant and takes steps to obtain a divorce, but before the case is ready for hearing is seized with scruples and gives up the attempt, chiefly because she fears she is influenced by an unholy love for Stuart. Finally she gets leave of absence from her amiable spouse, and dies of a broken heart before it expires, Stuart having married her dearest friend, the brilliant Lady Margaret Fordyce, thinking that Eleanor had no real affection for him.

The scruples are much to her credit, of course, but she might have tried to save the remainder of her life from the degradation which must have been the result of a reunion with her husband, yet kept aloof from Stuart without offending God or breaking any sacred law.

Eighteen very distinct characters figure in these pages, and three or four children. Of these the best drawn are those most lightly sketched. The author's favourites are too much described, their merits, their peculiarities, their faults (if allowed to have any) are detailed as the writer sees them. But they do not act and live and develop themselves to the reader, and, therefore, become abstractions, not living entities.

"Lost and Saved," written some dozen of years afterward, has much the same qualities as "Stuart of Dunleath." The subsidiary characters are more convincing than the leading ladies and gentlemen. The hero, if such a man could be so termed, with his extreme selfishness, his surface amiability, his infirmity of purpose and utter faithlessness, is well drawn. There is a respectable hero also, but we do not see much of him, which is not to be regretted, as he is an intolerable prig.

In this romance the heroine elopes with Treherne, the villainous hero. (Of course, there are the usual family objections to their wedding.) They intend to go to Trieste, but in the confusion of a night march they get on board the wrong steamer, and find themselves at Alexandria. Here Treherne is confronted with his aunt, the magnificent Marchioness of Updown. He is therefore obliged to suppress Beatrice (the heroine) until the Marchioness "moves on."

By MRS. ALEXANDER

They consequently set off on a voyage up the Nile, apparently in search of a clergyman to marry them. It seems, by the way, a curious sort of hunting-ground in which to track an English parson. Then Beatrice falls dangerously ill, and nothing will save her save a parson and the marriage service. A benevolent and sympathetic young doctor is good enough to simulate a British chaplain, and the knot is tied to the complete satisfaction of Beatrice. Much misery ensues.

It must be added that the magnificent Marchioness of Updown is an extraordinary picture. Besides being a peeress by marriage, she is the daughter of an earl, an aristocrat born and bred. Yet her vulgarity is amazing. Her stupid ill-nature, her ignorance, her speech and manner, suggest the idea of a small shopkeeper in a shabby street.

In this novel Mrs. Norton portrays the whited-sepulchre sort of woman very clearly in Milly, Lady Nesdale, who is admired and petted by Society, always smiling, well tempered, well dressed, careful to observe *les bienséances*, making herself pleasant even to her husband; while, screened by this fair seeming, she tastes of a variety of forbidden fruit, one mouthful of which would be enough to consign a less astute woman to social death. This class of character figures largely in present day novels, but few equal, none surpass, Mrs. Norton's masterly touch.

"Old Sir Douglas," her last novel, was published in *Macmillan's Magazine*, 1867. It is planned on the same lines as her previous works of fiction—the plot rather complicated, the characters extremely numerous; among these is an almost abnormally wicked woman who works endless mischief.

It was, however, as a poetess that Mrs. Norton was chiefly known. Her verse was graceful and harmonious, but more emotional than intellectual. Wrath at injustice and cruelty stirred the depths of her soul; her heart was keenly alive to the social evils around her and she longed passionately for power to redress them. The effect of her own wrongs and sufferings was to quicken her ardour to help her fellow women smarting under English law as it at that time existed. What that law then permitted is best exemplified by her own experience. When the legal proceedings between her and her husband were over, and her innocence of the charges brought against her was fully established, she was allowed to see her children only *once* for the space of half an hour in the presence of two witnesses chosen by Mr. Norton, though this state of things was afterwards ameliorated by the Infant Custody

Act, which allowed some little further restricted intercourse.

But these evil times are past. Indeed, it seems hard to believe that barely fifty years separates the barbarous injustice of that period from the decent amenities of this, as regards the respective rights of husbands and wives.

Mrs. Norton's second poem of importance, "The Undying One," is founded on the legend of the Wandering Jew, a subject always attractive to the poetic imagination. It contains many charming lines, and touches on an immense variety of topics, wandering, like its hero, over many lands. The sufferings of isolation are vividly depicted, and isolation must, of necessity, be the curse of endless life in this world.

> "Thus, thus, to shrink from every outstretched hand,
> To strive in secret and alone to stand,
> Or, when obliged to mingle in the crowd,
> Curb the pale lip which quiveringly obeys,
> Gapes wide with sudden laughter, vainly loud,
> Or writhes a faint, slow smile to meet their gaze.
> This, this is hell! the soul which dares not show
> The barbed sorrow which is rankling there,
> Gives way at length beneath its weight of woe,
> Withers unseen, and darkens to despair!"

In these days of rapidity and concentration, poems such as this would never emerge from the manuscript stage, in which they might be read by appreciative friends with abundant leisure.

The same observation applies to "The Dream." A mother sits watching the slumber of her beautiful young daughter who, waking, tells her dream of an exquisite life with the one she loves best, unshadowed by grief or pain. The mother warns her that life will not be like this, and draws a somewhat formidable picture of its realities. From this the girl naturally shrinks, wondering where Good is to be found, and is answered thus:

> "He that deals blame, and yet forgets to praise,
> Who sets brief storms against long summer days,
> Hath a sick judgment.
> And shall we *all* condemn, and *all* distrust,
> Because some men are false and some unjust?"

Some of Mrs. Norton's best and most impassioned verses are to be found in the dedication of this poem to her friend, the Duchess of Sutherland.

Affection, gratitude, indignation, grief, regret—*these* are the sources of Mrs. Norton's inspiration; but of any coldly intellectual solution of life's puzzles, such as more modern writers affect, there is little trace.

"The Lady of La Garaye" is a Breton tale (a true one) of a beautiful and noble Châtelaine, on whom Heaven had showered all joy and blessing. Adored by her husband, she shared every hour of his life and accompanied him in his favourite sport of hunting. One day she dared to follow him over too wide a leap. Her horse fell with and on her. She was terribly injured, and crippled for life. After much lamenting she is comforted by a good priest, and institutes a hospital for incurables, she and her husband devoting themselves to good works for the remainder of their days. The versification is smooth, the descriptions are graceful and picturesque; but neither the subject nor its treatment is enthralling.

Mrs. Norton's finest poetic efforts are to be found in her short pieces. One entitled "Ataraxia" has a soothing charm, which owes half its melody to the undertone of sadness which pervades the verse.

> "Come forth! The sun hath flung on Thetis' breast
> The glittering tresses of his golden hair;
> All things are heavy with a noon-day rest,
> And floating sea-birds cleave the stirless air.
> Against the sky in outlines clear and rude
> The cleft rocks stand, while sunbeams slant between
> And lulling winds are murmuring through the wood
> Which skirts the bright bay, with its fringe of green.
>
> "Come forth! all motion is so gentle now
> It seems thy step alone should walk the earth,
> Thy voice alone, the 'ever soft and low,'
> Wake the far haunting echoes into birth.

MRS. NORTON

Too wild would be Love's passionate store of hope,
Unmeet the influence of his changeful power,
Ours be companionship whose gentle scope
Hath charm enough for such a tranquil hour."

From the perusal of her writings, the impression given by her portrait, and the reminiscences of one who knew her, we gather an idea of this charming and gifted woman, whose nature seems to have been rich in all that makes for the happiness of others, and of herself. We feel that she possessed a mind abundantly stored, an imagination stimulated and informed by sojourning in many lands; a heart, originally tender and compassionate, mellowed by maternal love, a judgment trained and restrained by constant intercourse with the best minds of the period, a wit keen as a damascene blade, and a soul to feel, even to enthusiasm, the wrongs and sufferings of others.

Add to these gifts the power of swift expression, and we can imagine what a fascination Mrs. Norton must have possessed for those of her contemporaries who had the privilege of knowing her. "She was the most brilliant woman I ever met," said the late Charles Austen, "and her brilliancy was like summer lightning; it dazzled, but did not hurt." Unless, indeed, she was impelled to denounce some wrong or injustice, when her words could strike home. Yet to this lovely and lovable woman, life was a long disappointment; and through all she has written a strain of profound rebellion against the irony of fate colours her views, her delineations of character, her estimate of the social world. By her relations and friends she was warmly appreciated.

She did not succeed in obtaining the relief of divorce until about 1853. Mr. Norton survived till 1875, and in 1877, a few months before her death, his widow married Sir William Stirling-Maxwell.

It is a curious instance of the change of fashion and the transient nature of popular memory that great difficulty is experienced in obtaining copies of Mrs. Norton's works, especially of her poems. "The Undying One," "The Dream," and one or two smaller pieces, are found only in the British Museum Library. The novels are embedded in the deeper strata of Mudie's, but are not mentioned in the catalogue of that all-embracing collection. Yet forty years ago, Mrs. Norton acknowledged that she made at one time about £1400 a year by her pen, this chiefly by her contributions to the annuals of that time.

Mrs. Norton, however, had not to contend with the cruel competition which lowers prices while it increases labour. In her day, the workers were few, and the employers less difficult to please. But these comparisons are not only odious, but fruitless. The crowd, the competition, the desperate struggle for life, exists, increases, and we cannot alter it. We can but train for the contest as best we may, and say with the lovely and sorely tried subject of this sketch, as she writes in her poem to her absent boys:

> "Though my lot be hard and lonely,
> Yet I hope—I hope through all."

Annie Hector

("Mrs. Alexander")

"A. L. O. E." (MISS TUCKER)
MRS. EWING

By MRS. MARSHALL

"A. L. O. E." (MISS TUCKER)
MRS. EWING

Forty years ago, the mystic letters "A. L. O. E." ("A Lady of England") on the title-page of a book ensured its welcome from the children of those days. There was not then the host of gaily bound volumes pouring from the press to be piled up in tempting array in every bookseller's shop at Christmas. The children for whom "A. L. O. E." wrote were contented to read a "gift-book" more than once; and, it must be said, her stories were deservedly popular, and bore the crucial test of being read aloud to an attentive audience several times.

Many of these stories still live, and the allegorical style in which "A. L. O. E." delighted has a charm for certain youthful minds to this day. There is a pride and pleasure in thinking out the lessons hidden under the

"A. L. O. E." (MISS TUCKER)

names of the stalwart giants in the "Giant Killer," which is one of "A. L. O. E.'s" earlier and best tales. A fight with Giant Pride, a hard battle with Giant Sloth, has an inspiring effect on boys and girls, who are led to "look at home" and see what giants hold them in bondage.

"A. L. O. E.'s" style was almost peculiar to herself. She generally used allegory and symbol, and she was fired with the desire to arrest the attention of her young readers and "do them good." We may fear that she often missed her aim by forcing the moral, and by indulging in long and discursive "preachments," which interrupted the main current of the story, and were impatiently skipped that it might flow on again without vexatious hindrances.

In her early girlhood and womanhood "A. L. O. E." had written plays, which, we are told by her biographer, Miss Agnes Giberne, were full of wit and fun. Although her literary efforts took a widely different direction when she began to write for children, still there are flashes of humour sparkling here and there on the pages of her most didactic stories, showing that her keen sense of the ludicrous was present though it was kept very much in abeyance.

From the first publication of "The Claremont Tales" her success as a writer for children was assured. The list of her books covering the space of fifteen or twenty years is a very long one, and she had no difficulty in finding publishers ready to bring them out in an attractive form.

"The Rambles of a Rat" is before me, as I write, in a new edition, and is a very fair specimen of " A. L. O. E.'s " work. Weighty sayings are put into the mouth of the rats, and provoke a smile. The discussion about the ancestry of Whiskerando and Ratto ends with the trite remark—which, however, was not spoken aloud—that the great weakness of one opponent was pride of birth, and his anxiety to be thought of an ancient family ; but the chief matter, in Ratto's opinion, was not whether our ancestors do honour to us, but whether by our conduct we do not disgrace them. Probably this page of the story was hastily turned here, that the history of the two little waifs and strays who took shelter in the warehouse, where the rats lived, might be followed.

Later on there is a discussion between a father and his little boy about the advantage of ragged schools, then a somewhat new departure in philanthropy. Imagine a boy of nine, in our time, exclaiming, "What a glorious thing it is to have ragged schools and reformatories, to give the poor and the ignorant, and the wicked, a chance of becoming honest and happy." Boys of Neddy's age, nowadays, would denounce him as a little prig, who ought to be well

"A. L. O. E." (MISS TUCKER)

snubbed for his philanthropical ambition, when he went on to say, "How I should like to build a ragged school myself!" "The Voyage of the Rats to Russia" is full of interest and adventure, and the glimpse of Russian life is vivid, and in "A. L. O. E.'s" best manner.

Indeed, she had a graphic pen, and her descriptions of places and things were always true to life. In "Pride and his Prisoners," for instance, there are stirring scenes, drawn with that dramatic power which had characterised the plays she wrote in her earlier days. "The Pretender, a farce in two Acts, by Charlotte Maria Tucker," is published in Miss Giberne's biography. In this farce there is a curious and constantly recurring play on words, but the allegory and the symbol with which she afterwards clothed her stories are absent.

"A. L. O. E." did not write merely to *amuse* children; and the countless fairy tales and books of startling adventure, in their gilded covers and with their profuse illustrations, which are published every year, have thrown her stories into the shade. But they are written with verve and spirit, and in good English, which is high praise, and cannot always be given to the work of her successors in juvenile literature. In her books, as in every work she undertook throughout her life, she had the high and noble aim of doing good. Whether she might have widened the sphere of her influence by less of didactic teaching, and by allowing her natural gifts to have more play, it is not for us to inquire.

It is remarkable that this long practice in allegory and symbol fitted her for her labours in her latter years, amongst the boys and girls of the Far East. Her style was well adapted to the Oriental mind, and kindled interest and awoke enthusiasm in the hearts of the children in the Batala Schools. Here she did a great work, which she undertook at the age of fifty-four, when she offered her services to the Church Missionary Society as an unpaid missionary.

"All for love, and no reward" may surely be said to be "A. L. O. E.'s" watchword, as, with untiring energy, she laboured amongst the children in a distant part of the empire. Even there she was busy as an author. By her fertile pen she could reach thousands in that part of India who would never see her face or hear her voice. She wrote for India as she had written for England, ever keeping before her the good of her readers. The Hindu boys and girls, as well as the children of this country, have every reason to hold her name in grateful remembrance as one of the authors who have left a mark on the reign of Queen Victoria.

MRS. EWING

THERE lingers over some people whom we know a nameless charm. It is difficult to define it, and yet we feel it in their presence as we feel the subtle fragrance of flowers, borne to us on the wings of the fresh breeze, which has wandered over gorse and heather, beds of wild hyacinth, and cowslip fields, in the early hours of a sunny spring day. A charm like this breathes over the stories which Mrs. Ewing has left as an inheritance for English children, and for their elders also, for all time. The world must be better for her work; and looking back over the sometimes toilsome paths of authorship, this surely, above all others, is the guerdon all craftswomen of the pen should strive to win.

There is nothing morbid or melodramatic in Mrs. Ewing's beautiful stories. They bubble over with the joys of child-life; they bristle with its humour; they touch its sorrows with a tender, sympathetic hand; they lend a gentle sadness of farewell to Death itself, with the sure hope of better things to come.

It was in 1861 and 1862 that those who were looking for healthy stories for children found, in " Melchoir's

By MRS. MARSHALL

Dream and other Tales," precisely what they wanted. Soon after, *Aunt Judy's Magazine*, edited by Mrs. Ewing's mother, Mrs. Gatty, made a new departure in the periodical literature for children. The numbers were eagerly looked for month by month, and the title of the magazine was given to commemorate the "Judy" of the nursery, who had often kept a bevy of little brothers and sisters happy and quiet by pouring forth into their willing ears stories full of the prowess of giants, the freaks of fairies, with occasional but always good-natured shafts aimed at the little faults and frailties of the listening children.

Aunt Judy's Magazine had no contributions from Mrs. Ewing's pen till May 1866 and May 1867. Then the delightful "Remembrances of Mrs. Overtheway" enchanted her youthful readers. Little Ida's own story and her lonely childhood had an especial charm for them; and Mrs. Overtheway's remembrances of the far-off days when she, too, was a child, were told as things that had really happened. And so they had! For, in the disappointment of the imaginative child who had created a fair vision from her grandmother's description of Mrs. Anastasia Moss as a golden-haired beauty in rose-bud brocade, and instead, saw an old lady with sunken black eyes, dressed in *feuilles mortes* satin, many a child may have found the salient parts of her own experience rehearsed!

"Alas!" says Mrs. Overtheway, when little Ida, soothed by her gentle voice, has fallen asleep. "Alas! my grown-up friends, does the moral belong to children only? Have manhood and womanhood no passionate, foolish longings, for which we blind ourselves to obvious truth, and of which the vanity does not lessen the disappointment? Do we not all toil after rose-buds to find *feuilles mortes?*" It is in touches like this, in her stories, that Mrs. Ewing appeals to many older hearts as well as to those of the young dreamers, taking their first steps in the journey of life.

In 1857, Juliana Horatia Gatty married Alexander Ewing, A.P.D., and for some time "Mrs. Overtheway's Remembrances" were not continued. The last of them, "Kerguelin's Land," is considered by some critics the most beautiful of the series, ending with the delightful surprise of little Ida's joy in the return of her lost father.

Mrs. Ewing's stories are so rich in both humour and pathos, that it is difficult to choose from them distinctive specimens of her style, and of that charm which pervades them, a charm which we think is peculiarly her own.

Mrs. Ewing gave an unconsciously faithful portrait of

herself in "Madam Liberality." The reader has in this story glimpses of the author's own heroic and self-forgetful childhood. Perhaps this tale is not as well known as some which followed it: so a few notes from its pages may not be unwelcome here.

Madam Liberality, when a little girl, was accustomed to pick out all the plums from her own slice of cake and afterwards make a feast with them for her brothers and sisters and the dolls. Oyster shells served for plates, and if by any chance the plums did not go round the party, the shell before Madam Liberality's place was always the empty one. Her eldest brother had given her the title of Madam Liberality; and yet he could, with refreshing frankness, shake his head at her and say, "You are the most *meanest* and the *generousest* person I ever knew."

Madam Liberality wept over this accusation, and it was the grain of truth in it that made her cry, for it was too true that she screwed, and saved, and pinched to have the pleasure of "giving away." "Tom, on the contrary, gave away without pinching and saving. This sounds much handsomer, and it was poor Tom's misfortune that he always believed it to be so, though he gave away what did not belong to him, and fell back for the supply of his own pretty numerous wants upon other people, not forgetting Madam Liberality."

What a clever analysis of character is this! We have all known the "Toms," for they are numerous, and some of us have known and but scantily appreciated the far rarer "Madam Liberalitys."

It is difficult to read unmoved of the brave child's journey alone to the doctor to have a tooth taken out which had caused her much suffering. Then when about to claim the shilling from her mother, which was the accustomed reward for the unpleasant operation, she remembered the agreement was a shilling for a tooth with fangs, sixpence for a tooth without them. She did so want the larger sum to spend on Christmas presents; so, finding a fang left in her jaw, she went back to the doctor, had it extracted, and staggered home once more, very giddy but very happy, with the tooth and the fang safe in a pill box!

"Moralists say a great deal about pain treading so very closely on the heels of pleasure in this life, but they are not always wise or grateful enough to speak of the pleasure which springs out of pain. And yet there is a bliss which comes just when pain has ceased, whose rapture rivals even the high happiness of unbroken health.

"Relief is certainly one of the most delicious sensations which poor humanity can enjoy."

Madam Liberality often suffered terrible pain from

quinsy. Thus we read sympathetically of her heroic efforts one Christmastide, when nearly suffocated with this relentless disease, to go on with her preparations to get her little gifts ready for the family. And how we rejoice when a cart rumbles up to the door and brings a load of beautiful presents, sent by a benevolent lady who has known Madam Liberality's desire to make purchases for her brothers and sisters, and has determined to give her this delightful surprise.

The story of Madam Liberality, from childhood to maturity, is, we think, written in Mrs. Ewing's best manner, though, perhaps, it has never gained the widespread popularity of "Jackanapes," and "The Story of a Short Life," or "A Flat Iron for a Farthing."

Of the last-named story Mrs. Bundle is almost the central figure. In the childhood of Reginald Dacre, who writes his own reminiscences, she played a prominent part. Loyal and true, she held the old traditions of faithful service; her master's people were her people, and she had but few interests apart from them.

The portrait of Reginald's mother hung in his father's dressing-room, and was his resort in the early days of his childish sorrows. Once when his dog Rubens had been kicked by a guest in his father's house, Reginald went to that picture of his golden-haired mother and wept out his plaintive entreaties that "Mamma would come back to Rubens and to him—they were so miser-ra-ble." "Then," he says, "in the darkness came a sob that was purely human, and I was clasped in a woman's arms and covered with tender kisses and soothing caresses. For one wild moment, in my excitement and the boundless faith of childhood, I thought my mother had heard me and come back. But it was only Nurse Bundle!"

Then, passing over many years, when Reginald Dacre brought his bride to his old home, this faithful friend, after giving her loving welcome to the new Mrs. Dacre, went, in the confusion and bewilderment of old age, with its strange mingling of past and present, to the room where the portrait of her lost lady with the golden hair still hung; and there, the story goes on to say, "There, where years before she had held me in her arms with tears, I, weeping also, held her now in mine—quite dead!"

This is one of the most pathetic incidents in all Mrs. Ewing's works, told without the least exaggeration and with the simplicity which is one of the characteristics of her style.

"Lob Lie by the Fire" contains some of the author's brightest flashes of humour, and yet it closes with a description of Macalister's death, drawn with the tender hand with which that solemn mystery is ever touched by Mrs. Ewing, beautiful in its pathetic simplicity. Nothing in its way can be more profoundly touching than the few words which end this story :—

"After a while Macalister repeated the last word, '*Home*.' And as he spoke there spread over his face a smile so tender and so full of happiness that John Broom held his breath as he watched him. As the light of sunrise creeps over the face of some rugged rock, it crept from chin to brow, and the pale blue eyes shone, tranquil, like water that reflects heaven. And when it had passed, it left them still open—but gems that had lost their ray."

"Jackanapes" is so well known, almost the best known of the author's charming stories, that we will not dwell on the pathos of that last scene, when Jackanapes, like one in the old allegory, heard the trumpets calling for him on the other side—the gallant boy who had laid down his life for his friend. But the character of the Gray Goose, who slept securely with one leg tucked up under her on the green, is so delightfully suggestive that we must give some of her wisdom as a specimen of the author's humorous but never unkindly hits at the weaknesses to which we are all prone.

"The Gray Goose and the big Miss Jessamine were the

only elderly persons who kept their ages secret. Indeed, Miss Jessamine never mentioned any one's age, or recalled the exact year in which anything had happened. The Gray Goose also avoided dates. She never got farther than 'last Michaelmas,' 'the Michaelmas before that,' and 'the Michaelmas before the Michaelmas before that.' After this her head, which was small, became confused, and she said 'Ga-ga!' and changed the subject."

Then again :

"The Gray Goose always ran away at the first approach of the caravans, and never came back to the green till nothing was left of the fair but footmarks and oyster-shells. Running away was her pet principle; the only system, she maintained, by which you can live long and easily, and lose nothing.

"Why in the world should any one spoil the pleasures of life, or risk his skin, if he can help it?

'What's the use?
Said the goose.'

Before answering which one might have to consider what world, which life, and whether his skin were a goose skin. But the Gray Goose's head would never have held all that."

Major Ewing was stationed at Aldershot in 1869, and

during the eight years Mrs. Ewing lived there her pen was never idle. *Aunt Judy's Magazine* for 1870 was well supplied with tales, of which " Amelia " is perhaps one of the best.

To her life at Aldershot we owe the story which had for its motto " Lœtus sorte mea," and which is full of the most graphic descriptions of the huts and the soldiers' life in camp. As in the story of Madam Liberality we have glimpses of the author's childhood with all its little cares and joys, so in the " Story of a Short Life " we have the actual experience of a soldier's life in camp.

O'Reilly, the useful man of all trades, with his warm Irish heart, and his devotion to the Colonel's wife, his erratic and haphazard way of performing his duties, his admiration for the little gentleman in his velvet coat and lace collar, who stood erect by his side when the funeral passed to the music of the Dead March, imitating his soldierlike bearing and salute, is a vivid picture touched by the skilled hand of a word painter.

So also is the figure of the V.C., who in his first talk with the crippled child, stands before us as the ideal of a brave soldier, who sets but little store on his achievements, modest as the truly great always are, and encouraging the boy to fight a brave battle against irritable temper and impatience at the heavy cross of suffering laid upon him.

"'You are a V.C.,' Leonard is saying, 'and you ought to know. I suppose nothing—not even if I could be good always from this minute right away till I die—nothing could ever count up to the courage of a V.C.?'

"'God knows it could, a thousand times over,' was the V.C.'s reply.

"'Where are you going? Please don't go. Look at me. They're not going to chop the Queen's head off, are they?'

"'Heaven forbid! What are you thinking about?'

"'Why because—look at me again—ah! you've winked it away; but your eyes were full of tears, and the only other brave man I ever heard of crying was Uncle Rupert, and that was because he knew they were going to chop the poor king's head off.' That was enough to make anybody cry."

They were in the room where the picture of the young cavalier ancestor of Leonard hung. He always called him "Uncle Rupert," and he would meditate on the young face with the eyes dim with tears—eyes which always seemed to follow him, and, as he fancied, watched him sorrowfully, now no longer able to jump about and play with the Sweep, but lying helpless on his couch, or limping about on his crutches, often with pain and difficulty.

By MRS. MARSHALL

This conversation between the V.C. and Leonard was the beginning of a strong friendship which was put to the test one Sunday when Leonard lay dying in the hut of his uncle, the barrack-master.

The V.C. hated anything like display or bringing himself into notice. Thus it cost him something to take up his position outside the iron church in the camp, that Leonard might hear the last verses of the tug-of-war hymn. The V.C.'s attachment to his little friend triumphed over his dislike to stand alone singing,

> " The Son of God goes forth to war,
> A kingly crown to gain."

The melodious voice of the gallant young soldier rang through the air and reached the dying ears of little Leonard. The soldiers loved this hymn, and the organist could never keep them back. The soldiers, the story says, had begun to tug. In a moment more the organ stopped, and the V.C. found himself with over three hundred men at his back, singing without accompaniment and in unison:

> " A noble army, men and boys,
> The matron and the maid,
> Around the Saviour's throne rejoice
> In robes of white arrayed."

Even now, as the men paused to take breath after their "tug," the organ spoke again softly but seraphically. Clearer and sweeter above the voices behind him rose the voice of the V.C. singing to his little friend :

> "They climbed the steep ascent to Heaven
> Through peril, toil and pain."

The men sang on, but the V.C. stopped as if he had been shot. For a man's hand had come to the Barrack Master's window *and pulled down the blind!*

Here, again, we have an instance of this author's power to touch her readers, even to tears, by the true pathos which needs but few words to bring it home to many hearts.

Taken as a whole, "The Story of a Short Life" has, it may be, some faults of construction, which arose from its being written in detached portions. The history of St. Martin, though it is not without its bearing on the story of the beautiful and once active child's bruised and broken life, and his desire to be a soldier, rather spoils the continuity of the narrative.

"The Story of a Short Life" was not published in book form until four days before the author's death ; but it was not her last work, though from its appearance at that moment the title was spoken of by some reviewers as singularly appropriate.

By MRS. MARSHALL

Mrs. Ewing's love for animals may be seen in all her stories—Leonard's beloved "Sweep," Lillo the red-haired pony on which Jackanapes took his first ride, and the dog in the blind man's story dying of grief on his grave, are all signs of the author's affection for those who have been well called "our silent friends." Her own pets were indeed her friends—from a pink-nosed bulldog called Hector, to a refugee pup saved from the common hangman, and a collie buried with honours, his master making a sketch of him as he lay on his bier.

Mrs. Ewing was passionately fond of flowers, and "Mary's Meadow" was written in the last years of her life as a serial for *Aunt Judy's Magazine*. Her very last literary work was a series of letters from a Little Garden, and the love of and care for flowers is the theme.

Much of Mrs. Ewing's work cannot be noticed in a paper which is necessarily short. But enough has been said to show what was her peculiar gift as a writer for children.

It is sometimes said that to write books for children cannot be considered a high branch of literature. We venture to think this is a mistake. There is nothing more difficult than to arrest the attention of children. They do not as a rule care to be *written down* to—they can appreciate what is good and are pleased when their elders can enter into and admire the story which has interested and delighted them.

To write as Mrs. Ewing wrote is undoubtedly a great gift which not many possess, but a careful study of her works by young and old authors and readers alike cannot be without benefit. She was a perfect mistress of the English language; she was never dull and never frivolous. There is not a slip-shod sentence, or an exaggerated piling up of adjectives to be found in her pages. She knew what she had to say, and she said it in language at once pure, forcible, and graceful.

We must be grateful to her for leaving for us, and for our children's children, so much that is a model of all that tends to make the literature of the young—yes, and of the old also—attractive, healthy, and delightful.

Emma Marshall

www.ingramcontent.com/pod-product-compliance
Lightning Source LLC
Chambersburg PA
CBHW030751230426
43667CB00007B/929